The Hostile Environment

The Hostile Environment

Students Who Bully in School

Susan Carter

LEXINGTON BOOKS
Lanham • Boulder • New York • London

Published by Lexington Books
An imprint of The Rowman & Littlefield Publishing Group, Inc.
4501 Forbes Boulevard, Suite 200, Lanham, Maryland 20706
www.rowman.com

Unit A, Whitacre Mews, 26-34 Stannary Street, London SE11 4AB

British Library Cataloguing in Publication Information Available

Library of Congress Control Number: 2015952183
ISBN: 978-0-7391-9722-6 (cloth : alk. paper)
eISBN: 978-0-7391-9723-3

♾™ The paper used in this publication meets the minimum requirements of American National Standard for Information Sciences—Permanence of Paper for Printed Library Materials, ANSI/NISO Z39.48-1992.

Printed in the United States of America

Contents

Introduction[1]

Problems Associated With the Study of Bullying

School bullying is a persistent problem that destroys childhoods, families, and communities. Daily media reports of childhood suicides allegedly resulting from bullying capture the attention of societies across the globe. Unfortunately, these tragic events occur so frequently, the only differences are the date, name of the victim, and the particular school and country where it occurred. Checking the Internet at this moment, the United Kingdom's *Daily Mail* reports the suicide of 11-year-old Thomas Thompson who was bullied, had his life threatened with peer attempts to strangle him with his tie, and was called "gay boy" and "fatso." So often the case, the school's headmaster denied knowing of bullying or had knowledge of Thomas being treated differently, taking no responsibility for his suicide.

The topic of school bullying has been tackled by researchers, educators, mental health providers, criminologists, lawyers, politicians, the media, and medical professionals across the world, but it is not always regarded as a disgusting, horrific, and ugly behavior. Schools and parents admit to being horrified by bullying but under their noses, their children are commonly texting, "Look at that skank," "bitch," "retard," "fatty," "faggot," "LOL," "he's such a loser," "she's a whore" "you will never have friends . . . " Despite school codes of conduct as well as federal and state legislation, bullying is allowed to continue in schools, in homes, and in communities. As a society we are conflicted because while our entertainment exposes us to bad behavior in talk and reality shows and often condones it, bullying is regarded as an international health concern, morally unacceptable by society, and having lasting negative effects on both bullies' and victims' mental health, social and academic outcomes (Swearer and Hymel 2015). Bullying has come to occupy a prominent role in the national consciousness of most countries, including developing nations, with initial research conducted in Scandinavia, the Netherlands, the

United Kingdom, Canada, Australia, New Zealand, and Japan. Bullying is a major public health problem demanding the concerted and coordinated time and attention of health care providers, policy-makers and families (Srabstein and Levental, 2010).

Challenging to stop, bullying in schools often results in a hostile environment, harming students, their families, and interfering with the process of teaching and learning. Suicides of youth secondary to bullying prompted the majority of states in the nation to enact legislation requiring schools to increase training on bully prevention, provide reporting guidelines for educators, and implement interventions for students who bully and their victims. United States initiatives including the White House Anti-Bullying Conference led by the President, Department of Education, and the Department of Health and Human Services (2010), the StopBullying.gov website, and Project Aware Grants designed to increase awareness of mental health issues (www.SAMHSA.gov) are examples of federal attempts to combat the seriousness of the national bullying problem. The movie industry is also onboard with productions such as the award-winning documentary, *Bully*, directed by film producer Lee Hirsch, poignantly portraying how bullying touches the lives of five families while attempting to dispel the cliché that kids will be kids and also the hit film, *Mean Girls,* recently celebrating its 10th anniversary (Rosenbaum, 2014).

Aggression dominates society and appears to have lasting effects according to Pillemer et al. (2012). Qualitatively studying nursing home residents, researchers found five types of aggression including inappropriate sexual behavior, invasion of privacy or personal integrity, roommate issues, intentional verbal aggression, and unprovoked actions. Although few think about aggression in the elderly, it appears that bad behavior and bullying have longevity. Transparency in researching and writing about school bullying is necessary but a difficult task and needs to be approached from perspectives from many disciplines in order to triangulate findings. Now is the opportune time to evaluate if progress has been made as anniversaries of several federal laws are occurring.

FEDERAL LAWS RELATED TO SCHOOL BULLYING

Notable is the 40th anniversary of the Individuals with Disabilities Education Act, originally the Education for All Handicapped Children Act (EHA, P. L. 94–142) enacted by the United States Congress in 1975 and signed into law by President Gerald Ford. EHA was revised and renamed as Individuals with Disabilities Education Act in 1990 and then reauthorized IDEA 2004. Parts of this federal legislation have broad implications for students who are bullying and their victims because frequently students are identified as having a disability. The enactment of EHA demonstrated the beginning of efforts to end discrimination for those having disabilities in schools requiring all public schools accepting federal funds to provide equal access to education for children with physical and mental disabilities. Public schools were required to evaluate handicapped children and create an educational plan with parent input that would emulate as closely as possible the educational experience of nondisabled students. PL 94–142 also contained a provision that disabled students should be placed in the least restrictive environment allowing the maximum possible opportunity to interact with non-impaired students. Separate schooling may only occur when the nature or severity of the disability is such that instructional goals cannot be achieved in the regular classroom. The law also contained a due process clause that guarantees an impartial hearing to resolve conflicts between the parents of disabled children to the school system.

Also notable is the imminent reauthorization of the Elementary and Secondary Education Act (ESEA) also known as No Child Left Behind (NCLB). In July 2015, the Senate and House of Representatives passed their rewrites for its reauthorization with the intention of going before President Barack Obama in the fall for his signature. Strong bipartisan backing was shown for the reauthorization of the bill, now referred to as the "Every Child Achieves Act of 2015" (Camera, Education Week, 2015). Currently, amendments to this bill include a discussion of bullying. Also noted was the recent attempt and failure again of the Senate to pass the Lesbian, Gay, Bisexual, Transgender (LGBT) students' anti-bullying bill known as the Student Nondiscrimination Act (Baldash, 2015).

These two laws have served to reduce barriers for students with disabilities allowing them to be educated with peers in the least restrictive environment while being afforded a free appropriate public education (IDEA 2004) and continue to have measures of school accountability. In the grand scheme of things, schools have performed well over the last forty years, given that IDEA and NCLB are underfunded mandates. Significant progress has been made for many students with disabilities who are now typically first considered for education in their neighborhood schools, contrary to the old practices of institutionalization for many only fifty years ago.

Arguably, IDEA clearly mandates the provision of services for students with disabilities in accordance with their Individualized Education Programs (IEPs). The connection to bullying is significant in some cases impacting the identification and selection of interventions for victims and bullies if they qualify with one of the federal definitions of disability. Bullying, according to the research, is often associated with emotional disability (ED) often comorbid with attention deficit hyperactivity disorder (ADHD), conduct disorder, depression, and anxiety. Given the nature of ED, services should include mandated counseling and supplementary aids and services for the child to make progress in the school's general curriculum. Unfortunately, students with ED often have behaviors that interfere with their education, and they drop out indicating a strong need to research and revise how services are delivered for this population of students. Many students with ED need a more intense level of support than what is currently provided, including school-based psychiatric care, direct social-emotional instruction, and high levels of teacher involvement with parents. Additionally, students who bully have negative outcomes such as involvement in criminal behavior indicating the importance of communicating early with law enforcement agencies. Communication serves not to criminalize the child's behaviors, but to build trust and support for schools and families. Confidentiality issues, coupled with school's fears of litigation and mental health stigma act as deterrents and unfortunate roadblocks, making this process challenging for school districts. Educators, families, mental health providers, and law enforcement need to devise procedures to improve communication while respecting confidentiality and building trust.

States have a legal obligation in regard to bully prevention and reporting. Every state in the nation now has an anti-bullying law in effect including Montana, the last of the States to enact one. States such as the New York's Dignity for All Students Act (DASA, 2013) now mandate bullying, harassment, and discrimination workshops for teachers where school districts provide mandatory training on bully prevention and reporting.

The research field continues to debate how to define and measure bullying and victimization. While self and parental report are most frequently utilized by researchers, peer reporting may be a more reliable measure because peers are present in at least 85% of bullying incidents (Pepler, Craig and O'Connell 2010). Furthermore, the prevailing notion of many students engaging in bullying may be a faulty assumption with bullying and victimization continually involving the same individuals. Chan (2006) found that "serial bullies" named as perpetrators by multiple victims, accounted for nearly 70% of victim reports; other reports reflected "multiple victimization," with several perpetrators bullying the same individual. Outcomes are poor for those involved in bullying, ". . . the bully is in a superior position of dominance with the ability to coerce, and there is a dysfunctional element, because bullying is morally outrageous and chronic aggression a serious risk factor for maladjustment" (Rodkin, Espelage, and Hanish 2015).

Unfortunately, bullying still persists despite the implementation of school anti-bullying programs. Students are still afraid to come to school, administrators spend much of the school day resolving disciplinary issues related to bullying, and consequences such as suspension have little effect in changing bullying behavior. Despite efforts to alleviate bullying, parents sometimes resort to transferring their child to another district because of the schools failed attempts to curb their child's victimization. Additionally, research on victimization indicates significantly more serious effects than previously thought. Children who are victimized have a heightened risk of headaches (Gini, Pozzoli, Lenzi and Vieno 2014), elevated depression symptoms causing blunted cortisol response (Vaillancourt et al. 2011), and telomere erosion in response to bullying stress (Shalev et al. 2012). A British study found that exposure to bullying in childhood caused an increase in blood inflammation biomarkers and adipose tissue in later adulthood (Takizawa et al. 2015). Social pain and physical pain are shown to share a common neurological network, highlighting why it may be that physical pain is often short lived whereas social pain, for some, seems to last a lifetime (Vaillancourt, Hymel and McDougall 2010).

Reducing bullying can be regarded as part of civil and human rights movement that has been afforded to adults in the workplace for years. Unfortunately, "many bullied children find that their schools are hostile environments, but civil rights protections against harassment apply only to children who fall into protected classes, such as racial and ethnic minorities, students with disabilities, and victims of gender harassment or religious discrimination" (Cornell and Limber 2015, 333).

Although Columbine received media attention, "less prominent in the national news, in the same year, the U.S. Supreme Court (Davis v. Monroe County Board of Education, 1999) established that schools could be liable for failure to stop student to student sexual harassment" (Cornell and Limber 2015, 333). Schools, neglecting to report bullying are sometimes found liable in student suicide as in the case of a 13-year-old Kentucky student who after repeated abuse, taunting and bullying, took his own life (Wolfson 2015). Students who are lesbian, gay and bisexual are at high risk for being bullied. A longitudinal study of bullying of sexual-minority youth from Alabama, Texas, and California while in 5th grade and later in the 7th and 8th grades was conducted. Consistent with prior research, sexual-minority youth experienced higher levels of bullying across grades with bullying declining with age, implying that students as early as 5th grade should be screened for bullying experiences (Schuster and Bogart 2015).

Research suggests poor outcomes for students who perpetrate bullying in school with bullying a significant predictor of violence later in life (Ttofi, Farrington and Losel 2011). Despite years of scholarly research, some schools choose interventions lacking efficacy. Research suggests effectiveness of anti-bullying programs increases with intensity and includes parent meetings, intense teacher training, school and classroom rules, firm disciplinary methods and improved playground supervision (Ttofi and Farrington. 2009,

2011). Unfortunately, few anti-bullying programs include models of parental involvement (Gross, Breitenstein, Eisback, Hope and Harrison, 2014). Also, in schools, the intensity and longevity of anti-bullying programs are often hampered due to stringent state and local curricular mandates and assessment processes and lack of funds. Duchnowski et al. (2012) found "schools that educate children who have ED appear to have an array of services to promote parent involvement in their child's education, and there are numerous federal policies promoting the involvement of parents in their child's education as an important contributor to their child's success. In the case of parents of children who have ED, there is a discrepancy between availability of service and engagement by parents in activities aimed to promote their involvement. Although schools attended by 71% of the students reported offering at least one type of family involvement activity, teachers reported only 17% of families of children with ED received a parent support service. The current challenge facing the field is to develop practices with effective content and mechanisms that would result in increased family engagement."

Additionally, initiatives addressing bullying often stress intervention for students who are victims, but do not outline specifics on supports for students who bully. A recent study in Brazil found the prevalence of aggressors in bullying situations was 20.8%, they were predominantly male, reported feeling lonely, experiencing insomnia, missing classes frequently, were exposed to domestic violence, smoked more tobacco and used more alcohol and illicit drugs than students who did not bully (Oliveira et al. 2015). This study suggests mental distress is present in those who bully and their victims, indicating a need to intervene with mental health initiatives. Research suggests a more intense approach, including the assessment of psychiatric problems in any children involved in bullying (Kumpulainen 2009). Research indicates bullying should be studied from a relational framework considering its form of aggression operates within relationships of power and abuse (Rodkin, Espelage, and Hanish 2015).

Many questions remain to be answered. What causes a child to bully, and what are the explanatory or mediating factors involved? Additionally, what moderating, mitigating, or exacerbating factors are involved? Why as a society do we allow children to be bullied relentlessly without substantial objections, indignation, adequate intervention, or outrage until the final act of suicide? (Coloroso 2003, xxi). What makes some excellent teachers and school districts indifferent to the child who incessantly bullies peers and sometimes adults? Why does a student who bullies get away with years of victimizing others while continuing to be a popular student and well-liked by teachers? Are teachers still afraid to get involved? As a society, what are our ethical obligations to children who bully and those who are the 1 to 5% that will exhibit very deviant behavior later on in life? Do we only provide services to the "nice" children who are victimized in school? Does stigma exist and is there resistance to the provision of mental health resources for only those who "deserve" them? Aren't schools obligated to protect children from harm? Are children faring better with anti-bullying programs and do they feel safe from bullying in school? Are children who bully and their victims experiencing improved mental health? Have student suicides secondary to bullying decreased?

Current students, enrolled in teacher college teacher preparation programs and practicing educators taking mandated anti-bullying workshops, share their anonymous accounts in later chapters and describe the bullying in their teaching positions and bullying events during their early school days. Many admitted to being haunted by the victimization years later. Concerns echo about what has been said for more than half a century; bullying is rampant and persistent in schools. Concerns as a teacher, administrator, and college professor, prompted the writing of this book with the intent of honestly and unemotionally presenting current issues and research from the many disciplines studying bullying. As a 21-year-old physical education teacher, and later as an administrator dealing with disciplinary issues, parents, teachers, and lawyers, I have seen bullying first-hand. Interventions may not be effective in changing the persistent, chronic bullying behavior of some children who bully and some children will be victimized throughout their school years. These children will have poor outcomes as adults and their lives will affect their families, their communities, and society. Observing children in various unstructured settings and working with teachers and families, I have witnessed the complexity of bullying with parents having children who persistently and subtlely bully their peers including kindergarteners who skillfully lie about their behaviors. Parents often deny their child's behaviors while teachers sometimes hold a child in high regard, frequently missing the bullying incidences in the classroom. Other teachers are aware of bullying behaviors and cannot be bothered to deal with them. I have seen administrators who are afraid of parents with attorneys, had conversations with parents who bully each other in neighborhoods, and both very poor and very affluent parents neglecting their children's bullying behavior. Parents have shared experiences where their child has been bullied relentlessly and who has been spit on and teased over several school years resulting in the decision to move their family so their child could start in another school district to avoid further harassment. I have seen the "flat affect" of some who have given up hope that adults will do something to help them and children with emotional disabilities sent to "appropriate" out-of-district schools who are forgotten by their neighborhoods, schools, and parents. I have seen bullies who are ringleaders, getting peers to join in their "serial" bullying behaviors year after year. Are these children part of the 1 to 5% of students who will need intense remediation and will they be resistant to social skills training and any kind of intervention?

I have concerns about the lack of persistence of anti-bullying programs and lack of intensity of school-based counseling for children who bully and their victims. I have concerns about teachers and paraeducators who do not want to be involved and will not report what they know despite new state laws. I have concerns about administrators who fail to report because parents of the bully are litigious or politically connected, or the student is an athlete, or they do not want their school to be marked as violent. I have concerns about the lack of understanding teachers have about students who bully, holding on to the prevailing myth of having poor self-esteem and low peer status. I worry about all the children who today are questioning their sexuality, or have disabilities and are being bullied, and dread getting on the bus every day, and dread everyday of their young lives. I worry about preschool teachers, parents and pediatricians who do not pay attention to bullying and aggressive behaviors in three- and four-year-olds. I have concerns about the shame and embarrassment many parents feel about discussing mental health problems with educators or other parents. And most of all, I feel for the all the students who are bullies and victims and are clearly in trouble emotionally. I am horrified that no one steps forward, is persistent enough or pays enough attention to the depression, anxiety, and other red flags that exist well before a student's suicide. I am concerned that agencies do not work together or collaborate with educators on students with mental health issues and manifesting severe behaviors. I am concerned that schools are not better equipped to deal with the 1 to 5% of our student population needing intense behavioral supports and counseling. I am worried that without preventative intervention, these students will end up exhibiting criminal behavior and callous-unemotional traits later on in life. Efforts to stop bullying needs to be more intense, with research available to educational administrators, policy makers influencing laws and educational initiatives, mental health providers, teachers, parents, and law enforcement.

Examining broad multidisciplinary research evidence is important and essential to the success of reducing school bullying. More attention needs to be devoted to the examination of the science rather than the attention given to the often emotional and reactive views of the media. Analyzing the bullying research, Bradshaw (2015) concludes that although bullying prevention programs can be effective in reducing bullying, there is a "great need for more work to increase the acceptability, fidelity and sustainability of the existing programs in order to improve bully-related outcomes for youth" (322). Findings are mixed on the effectiveness of school anti-bullying programs and as a result, school administrators are unclear as to what approaches if any have efficacy. The use of the public health model commonly used in schools and referred to response-to-intervention (Rtl) may be promising although few anti-bullying programs have procedures to deliver the intense intervention and counseling for children who bully and are bullied (Swearer, Wang, Collins, Strawhun and Fluke 2014). Research needs to guide national and state policy and the selection of efficacious interventions and programs in schools.

Bully prevention programs must consider the bully dynamic as a stressful event causing psychosocial difficulties. Examining individual characteristics and risk and protective factors to promote healthier relationships is also important. Expanding the lens to what is referred to as a diathesis-stress model where a child involved as a bully or victim, mixed with cognitive, biological and social vulnerabilities (i.e., diatheses) leads to internalizing and externalizing psychopathology (Swearer and Hymel 2015, p. 347) may be promising.

Bullying has received worldwide attention, but the challenge is to develop public health policies for bullying prevention including community awareness campaigns that are monitored by periodic assessment of the prevalence of bullying-related morbidity and mortality (Srabstein and Levental 2010). Every child has the right to feel safe alongside peers and every child who bullies needs intervention without question, without shame, and without blame. Bully prevention can reduce disruption in schools, reduce costs to society, and lead to healthier and happier lives. "Being bullied is not a harmless rite of passage but throws a long shadow over affected people's lives. Interventions in childhood are likely to reduce long-term health and social costs" (Wolke et al. 2013, 1).

Strategies to eradicate bullying should combine education, school-based interventions, and policy reform leading to cultural change where policymakers and legislators affirm that public education is a right for all students and bullying is an impediment to that right (Cornell and Limber 2015). Mental health of children, particularly those with more intense needs is recognized as a serious concern. School mental health (SMH) initiatives should address the significant gap between youth who need and youth who receive mental health supports. As many as 20% of children and youth require multifaceted academic/behavior and mental health supports which the usual systems within education and mental health have not routinely provided (Eber et al. nd).

Although society's outrage is palpable and bullying incidences are reported daily by the media the outrage is not enough. Research consistently supports that the number of students who bully and who are victims is large, despite worldwide efforts to reduce it. Children have a right to feel safe in school, and a right to be supported emotionally if mental health interferes with their learning. Communities and local governance need to consult the research and make smart decisions in order to change what has occurred over the last fifty years.

HISTORY OF SCHOOL BULLYING RESEARCH

The research base on bullying began in Scandinavia during the late 1960s and early 1970s when Daniel Olweus, a Swedish psychologist and colleagues found 15% of children involved in bullying, with 6% classified as bullies (1993). His book, written in 1978 (original Swedish version 1973) is the seminal publication to bring bullying to the forefront to the educational and scientific community (Smith, 2000). In Norway during the 1980's, three boys committed suicide after being bullied by peers triggering a national campaign against bullying and the development of the Olweus Bullying Prevention Program (Olweus, Limber and Mihalic, 1999). Researchers in Europe and the United States followed and began examining bullying as a group process in the 1990s. Crick, a U.S. researcher introduced the concept of relational aggression as a subtype of bullying particularly evident among girls (Crick and Grotpeter, 1995). Salmivalli et al. (1996) from Finland began studying the group process of bullying publishing extensively to the present day.

The word bullying, now commonplace in the English vernacular, originated in the middle of the sixteenth century from the Dutch word *boele*, meaning lover (as cited in Smith 2000). Contrary to this definition, bully perpetration, the antithesis of endearment, is an aggressively planned act, while perpetration, derived from the Latin verb *perpetrare*, is defined as an act of committing. Bullying is persistent, proactive and recognized as a relationship problem involving repeated hostile actions taking place within a relationship characterized by a power differential (Olweus 1993; Pepler and Craig 2000), differing from isolated, transitory interpersonal conflicts in that it involves systematic, intentional, prolonged and repeated negative attacks aimed at a person (Mikkelson and Einarsen 2002). Specifically,

A student is bullied or victimized when he or she is exposed repeatedly and over time to negative actions on the part of one or more other students. Bullies are skilled at hiding their behavior from adults, show little empathy for those they target, have average to better than average self-esteem, and possess a need to feel powerful and dominate others. Children who bully learn that power and aggression lead to attention, dominance, and increased status of some of their peers and being aggressive can help you get what you want (Olweus 1993, 9).

SCHOOL SHOOTINGS AND CORRELATION TO BULLYING

Childhood aggression has been a societal concern for many years, but in the United States, since the tragic shootings at Columbine in 1999, significant concern and attention have been placed on school bullying. The suspected relationship to bullying prompted the United States Department of Education and Secret Service to investigate 41 school shooters and although no individual profile of characteristics was found, "Almost three-quarters of the attackers felt persecuted, bullied, threatened, attacked, or injured by others prior to the incident" (Vossekuil, et al. 2002, 21–22).

> In several cases, individual attackers had experienced bullying and harassment that was long-standing and severe. In some of these cases, the experience of being bullied seemed to have a significant impact on the attacker and appeared to have been a factor in his decision to mount an attack at the school. In one case, most of the attacker's schoolmates described the attacker as 'the kid everyone teased.' In witness statements from that incident, schoolmates alleged that nearly every child in the school had at some point thrown the attacker against a locker, tripped him in the hall, held his head under water in the pool or thrown things at him. Several schoolmates had noted that the attacker seemed more annoyed by, and less tolerant of, the teasing than usual in the days preceding the attack (Vossekuil, et al. 2002, 21–22).

School shootings prompted a study called The Safe School Initiative where the pre-attack behaviors of 37 school violence events in the United States from December 1974 through May 2000 were researched. Results led to the creation of *Threat Assessment in Schools: A Guide to Managing Threatening Situations and to Creating Safe School Climates* (Fein et al. 2004), a product involving collaboration between the United States Secret Service and the United States Department of Education. Threat assessment involves efforts to identify, assess, and manage individuals and groups who may pose threats of targeted violence. The guide focuses on the use of the threat assessment process as one component of the Department of Education's efforts to help schools across the nation reduce school violence, and create safe climates. Findings from this study also suggest red flags in some of the individual shooters existed well before the violence occurred, with those close to the shooter aware and concerned about atypical behaviors. Although behaviors are often recognized by parents, teachers, and mental health providers, poor integration of mental health resources and educational services, and poor communication between parents and educators, results in the overall failure of intervening efforts to meet the individual's needs. Welton, Vakil and Ford (2014) argue there is an inability to curb mass shooting and rampage school violence in schools across the United States, calling for more than anti-bullying programs, disciplinary measures, increased law security, with a more collaborative and interdisciplinary approach toward prevention. Bullying is a complicated event and some suggest perpetrators of school shootings not only experienced bullying from peers but also had different types of strain including home and family conflicts, feelings of isolation and a fatalistic sense of no future (Levin and Madfis 2009).

Although school shootings had a significant impact on decisions related to school safety, the perception that homicides in schools are common occurrences and schools are unsafe is inaccurate. Specifically, Nekvasil, Cornell, and Huang (2015) examining homicide incidents from 2005 through 2010, found despite public perceptions and media attention, multiple casualty shootings are more common in residences (47%) compared to schools (0.8%). Research suggests programs involving counseling, research-based anti-bullying programs and the use of threat assessment where multidisciplinary school-based teams use a decision tree to take a problem-solving approach may be more effective than expensive safety measures such as sophisticated surveillance systems, elaborate lockdown drills, and bulletproof glass.

CYBERBULLYING

Technological advances over the last decade have caused bullying to evolve. Cyber or electronic bullying via social media offers students ease, anonymity, and vast capability to cyberbully peers. As a result, new definitions of bullying now include cyberbullying.

> Bullying is characterized by aggression used within a relationship where the aggressor(s) has more real or perceived power than the target, and the aggression is repeated, or has the potential to be repeated, over time. Bullying can involve overt physical behavior or verbal, emotional, or social behaviors (*e.g.,* excluding someone from social activities, making threats, withdrawing attention, destroying someone's reputation) and can range from blatant aggression to far more subtle and covert behaviors. Cyber bullying or bullying through electronic technology (*e.g.,* cell phones, computers, online/social media), can include offensive text messages or e-mails, rumors or embarrassing photos posted on social networking sites, or fake online profiles (United States Department of Education, 2013).

The tragic suicides of many youth who have been bullied and the role of mass media in drawing attention to the issue has triggered individual states to create school-mandated anti-bullying laws including specific language on preventing and reporting cyberbullying. Although some forms of bullying are reportedly decreasing (Finkelhor, Turner et al. 2013), research indicates cyberbullying increased from 6% in 2000 to 11% in 2010 (Jones, Mitchell and Finkelhor, 2013) with social and verbal bullying the more common forms (Vaillancourt, Trink et al. 2010). As the technology evolves so does bully perpetration as reported in a recent segment on All Things Considered

(Siegel, 2015), a National Public Radio program. Some schools are buying an app called STOPit allowing students to anonymously report and stop cyberbullying. Inspired after the suicide of Amanda Todd, a 15-year-old who had been bullied online for about two years, this app allows a student to take a screenshot of anything seen on an electronic device and then send it to school officials as evidence. Additionally, the app, Yik Yak, used by some individuals to post anonymous suicidal thoughts (Shahani, 2015) can be used by anyone within a 5-mile radius to respond to cries for help anonymously. Although the app still is used on college campuses for hook-ups, gossip and rumors, there are reports this app is also used to express kindness, caring and support for those expressing the need for help. Counselors are urging Yik Yak users to encourage those who need help to get it.

Cyberbullying may be more dangerous than traditional bullying because youth have the ability to adapt quickly to the new device. The potential for cyberbullying increases with the advent of each new technology, computer network system, and electronic device that young people use to communicate. It can disrupt the school environment even if it occurs offsite because text and images are available to audiences 24 hours a day (Carter 2015). Interestingly, cyberbullying, while receiving much public attention, may not be more harmful compared to traditional forms of bullying. Mitchell et al. (2015) tested the role of technology in peer harassment and questioned whether it amplifies harm for youth. The belief that technology-based harassment has features that amplify emotional impact was not supported in this study. "In-person bullying and harassment was found to be more common and more distressing than harassment that solely occurs through technology" (p. 10). Victims subjected to both technology-based and in-person harassment had the most emotionally distressing of feelings of all, experiencing anger, sadness, and lack of trust.

PROBLEMS IN UNIFORMITY OF DEFINITIONS AND OPERATIONALIZING SUBTYPES OF BULLYING

Initially, researchers grouped children into one of two groups, bullies or victims. Some studies frame bullying by the person involved such as the bully perpetrator (pure bully, aggressor, victimizer), bully-victim (bully and victim, largely reactive to being bullied), victim (target, victimized), and bystander (noninvolved). Because of the problems in the uniformity of definitions and operationalizing the subtypes of bullying, researchers recognize the limitations of many research studies. Meta-analyses, although contributing to the literature base, have limitations in the generalization of results because of problems in uniformity of operationalizing bullying subtypes and defining it.

Other studies examine bullying by type including covert (relational aggression, exclusion, spreading rumors) and overt (verbal and physical abuse). Researchers question if bullying is distinctly separate from aggression and violence. Peer harassment, on the other hand is a broad term that includes bullying but also includes other types of interpersonal aggression that do not meet the standard definition of bullying because they do not involve repetition and power imbalances (Finkelhor, Turner, and Hamby, 2012, 1). Cook et al. (2010) argue that conceptual clarifications be made between serious violence, general aggression and bullying in order to add precision to the measurement of these behaviors.

Lack of uniformity in defining bullying prompted the Centers for Disease Control (CDC) to develop a uniform definition of bullying among youth as, "any unwanted aggressive behavior(s) by another youth or group of youths who are not siblings or current dating partners that involves an observed or perceived power imbalance and is repeated multiple times or is highly likely to be repeated. Bullying may inflict harm or distress on the targeted youth including physical, psychological, social, or educational harm."

THEORETICAL FRAMEWORKS USED TO STUDY BULLYING

Bullying is also studied through biological, behavioral, psychological, psychiatric, or educational lenses. Generally, the literature base considers bullying from several theoretical frameworks. Liu and Graves (2011) describe bullying from the ethological perspective where it serves as a tool for social dominance. The ecological and socio-ecological framework focuses on how the social environment affects individual behavior and includes factors such as school policies and social norms. Swearer and Espelage (2004) describe the bullying dynamic as more than the child who perpetrates but part of a larger social-ecological system with the interplay of individual, family, peer, school, and community contexts.

Another theory includes the cognitive and social-cognitive framework, considering an individual's characteristics such as impulsivity, antisocial tendencies, and the way they process information. Considering the influence of biological and genetics and how they influence aggression and violence has also been a lens to look at bullying.

A developmental psychopathology framework, where psychological and behavioral dysfunctions occurring in mental disorders, has also been used to study bullying. The intent is to improve the early identification and prevention of emotional and behavioral disorders (Forness 2003) suggesting educators need to understand psychiatric comorbidity and psychopharmacology especially when added to school behavioral intervention. Although special and general educators do not make medical or pharmacological suggestions for students, it is important that higher education training programs include coursework in these areas to increase prospects for accurate identification and appropriate interventions for increasing populations of psychiatrically challenged youth.

Crothers and Kolbert (2008) suggest viewing bullying as a behavior management issue where teachers spend "long periods of time observing their students in a variety of settings (e.g., classrooms, playground, lunchroom) as well as engaging in periodic retraining in conducting accurate observations and reliability checks (e.g., comparing perceptions with another teacher)" (133). Observation of students especially in unstructured settings is underutilized by teachers and left to behavior specialists, contracted to work with schools. Additionally recommended are constructive conversations with children who bully affirming their strengths and popularity. Furthermore, since parents often deny their child's behavior, using a no-nonsense, factual presentation of events while explaining decreased popularity among peers as a possible consequence of their child's bullying behavior may be effective. Unfortunately, sustained and expanded uses of interventions and practices have not been consistent or widespread (Sugai and Horner 2006). The practice of school-wide positive behavior support (SWPBS) emphasizes the integration of measurable outcomes, data-based decision-making, evidence-based practices, and overt support systems for implementers.

Exploring the research can offer different perspectives leading to the implementation of appropriate research-based interventions in schools. Without understanding how bullying presents, tighter school anti-bullying laws may not have the intended effect of reducing school bullying.

NOTE

1. Publisher's Note: The interviews used as supplemental research in this text were all conducted with the participants' knowledge and agreement that these interviews would be used in a later publication.

Chapter 1

Persistence of the Bullying Problem in Schools

Bullying is a common occurrence in schools and persists for many different reasons. Schools erroneously assume that anti-bullying programs are operating successfully, but research suggests otherwise. Research consistently indicates programs in school are too little, too late. Children who bully and children who are victims are not getting the intense interventions they need, are getting them too late, and school behavioral practices are ineffective and archaic. Frequency data indicates children who bully and those who are victimizing still occur at high rates.

FREQUENCY OF SCHOOL BULLYING

Nansel et al. (2001) conducting prevalence studies in the United States found 19% of students reporting bullying others, with greatest frequency in grades six through eight and at similar rates in urban, suburban, and rural schools. Nearly 21% of children were physically bullied, 53.6% verbally bullied, 51.4% socially bullied, and 13.6% electronically bullied (Wang et al. 2009) while 32% of children are bullied across 38 countries (World Health Organization 2012). Furthermore, bullying persists with close to 10% of adolescents consistently found to bully others over seven years (Pepler et al. 2008). One of three children in the United States is now reported to be effected by bullying, prompting the American Academy of Pediatrics (2011) to recommend pediatric screenings for bullying risk. Luxenberg, Limber, and Olweus (2014) studying a large data set of schools, found 15% of students reported being bullied two to three times a month or more, while 6% reported bullying others. Bullying involvement was highest among 3rd graders (23%) dropping to 15% in 7th grade and 8% in 12th grade, with 39% of the sample reporting bullying lasting for one year or longer. Males bullied more than females but the percentage difference was only 1 or 2% points until 9th grade when male bullying increased into the 12th grade. Verbal bullying, spreading rumors, and exclusion were most common types reported while bullying was most prevalent on playgrounds/athletic fields, lunchrooms and hallways/stairwells. Cyberbullying, occurring more in high school, was one of the least common methods used to bully in girls (6%) and boys (4%). The percentage of boys (18%) and girls (18%) involved in bullying was the same in grades three through 12, with girls (3%) and boys (4%) bullying peers. Unfortunately, high school students reported teachers were nearly twice as likely as elementary teachers to do little or nothing to reduce bullying. Ninety-three percent of girls and 81% of boys felt empathy toward those being bullied, but few reported reaching out to help. These data suggest more focus be placed on bullying by females as well as males occurring especially during the early elementary years, and empowering bystanders to come forward while improving teachers' abilities to intervene.

Results are mixed as to whether bullying has declined, but studies provide evidence that it presents differently. Studying trends in bullying among adolescents in the United States, Perlus et al. (2014) found 7.5% of students reporting bullying another person and 10.2% being victimized. Bully perpetration declined (more for middle school compared to high school students), and mostly in boys. While physical fighting decreased, weapon-carrying increased, especially in White students, despite White students having the greatest declines in bullying. The study found most common types of bullying were name-calling and social exclusion with boys having higher rates of bullying in all categories compared to girls, with the exception of social exclusion.

PROBLEMS WITH EXISTING SOCIETAL NORMS AND THE SELF-ESTEEM MISCONCEPTION

Bullying persists because societal norms continue to provide positive social and psychological reinforcement for bullying behavior (Greene 2000) although recent media campaigns responding to domestic violence exist (nomore.org). Additionally, the public and many educators continue to believe a student who bullies has low self-esteem. In a recent anti-bullying workshop, nearly 90% of practicing educators believed that a child bullies because of poor self-esteem. If teachers continue to have this misconception, and if bullying continues to go unchecked, the cost to society is significant. Research suggests that being a bully increases the risk of later violence in life by about two-thirds (Ttofi, Farrington and Lösel 2012) and also significantly raises the likelihood of being convicted of a criminal offense as an adult, of drug use, and of low job status compared to noninvolved peers (Farrington and Ttofi 2011; Olweus 1997; Sourander et al. 2006; Ttofi et al. 2011).

COMORBIDITY WITH PSYCHIATRIC DISORDERS NOT RECOGNIZED BY EDUCATORS

Teacher-training programs often require minimal coursework in psychology resulting in educators having a limited understanding of common childhood psychiatric disorders. Children who chronically bully others, coupled with possible psychiatric comorbidities are rarely considered in the development of anti-bullying programs despite state legislation mandating teacher-training workshops to provide coursework on "red flags" and indicators of bullying behavior among children. Additionally, scholarly research on predictors of bully perpetration is often not made available to educators.

PROBLEMATIC REFERRALS TO SPECIAL EDUCATION

Students in school with bullying behaviors and other emotional problems are frequently referred for special education evaluation, however the child frequently demonstrates significant acting out behaviors, numerous disciplinary referrals and suspensions before this referral takes place. Additionally the process of response-to-intervention (RtI) used to screen and collect behavioral data on students is sometimes (and sometimes illegally) used to delay the need for special education evaluations. These inappropriate and reactionary practices exacerbate bullying behaviors, causing significant harm to all involved. Additionally, problems exist during the referral and evaluation process when school districts urge parents to fund psychiatric evaluations through their medical insurance rather than incurring district expense, often resulting in delays. Reactive practices hurt all students, teachers, as well as taxpayers because often the child not provided with timely services ends up in a costly residential school setting. Increasing proactive responses to individual bullying will improve educational climate, benefit the child, and be cost-effective.

QUESTIONABLE POSITIVE EFFECTS OF ANTI-BULLYING PROGRAMS

Anti-bullying programs have effectively increased the awareness of bullying in schools and the community, however research results are mixed on their efficacy in reducing bullying. Merrill et al. (2008) conducting a meta-analysis, found anti-bullying interventions to be more likely to influence knowledge, attitudes, and self-perceptions rather than actual bullying behaviors, with the majority of outcome variables not meaningfully impacted. Others also found anti-bullying programs to have minimal effects of reducing bullying (Smith et al. 2004; Swearer et al. 2010). Furthermore, studies consistently demonstrate that children at risk for bullying are not likely to respond to anti-bullying programs (Rahey and Craig 2002; Hilton, Anngela-Cole and Wakita 2010) and need treatment related to personality disorders in childhood and adolescence. Many educators erroneously assume that teaching empathy and using other pro-socialization approaches will reduce bullying behaviors of students who chronically bully others but research suggests otherwise. A social-ecological framework of bullying considering the effects of "families, schools, peer groups, teacher-student relationships, parent-child relationships, parent-school relationships, neighborhoods and cultural expectations needs to be considered" (Swearer et al. 2010, 42).

Contrary to these findings, some meta-analyses do demonstrate positive effects of programs. Vreeman and Carroll (2007) found whole-school programs reduced bullying more often than curriculum-based or social skills training programs while Ttofi and Farrington (2011) found bullying and victimization decreased, finding a relationship between success and the program duration and intensity, parent-training meetings, firm disciplinary methods, consequences for children who bully, and improved playground supervision. Peer intervention actually resulted in an *increase* in bullying especially with "delinquent" children, agreeing with other research demonstrating poor effects of peer mediation.

Some researchers recommend more efforts in the implementation of effective programs with individual bullies and victims, based on child skills training programs (Losel and Beelman 2003). According to Smith et al. (2012), schools do have difficulty implementing anti-bullying policies. They found that schools did not mention important aspects of bullying in their policies including cyberbullying, bullying related to religion, gender preference, responsibilities of those aside from teaching staff, follow-up of incidents, and bullying to and from school. Results indicated schools struggled to formulate appropriate policies and are not sufficiently reactive in including strategies to prevent bullying. Overall, the study found school policies were unlikely to impact much on levels of bullying.

STIGMATIZING VIEW TOWARD STUDENTS WITH EMOTIONAL, BEHAVIORAL, AND PSYCHIATRIC DISORDERS

Society's attitudes have improved significantly over the past several decades since eugenics and the institutionalization of children and adults with mental disabilities, but stigma and lack of understanding still exists. The increasing need for mental health services is evident not only in schools, but throughout all aspects of society. Parental involvement in efforts to gain rights and services for children with autism and other disabilities has changed the landscape of how educational services are delivered, but significant stigma still exists for children with emotional disorders (ED) and associated mental health issues. Duplicating efforts of parents and advocacy groups responsible for the many autism initiatives, including advocacy, policy making and services may provide guidelines for enhancing mental health supports for children who bully. Parents are often reluctant to have their child evaluated or resistant to sharing their child's psychiatric diagnosis with family members or educators. Additionally, parents of some cultures are very sensitive to differences in their child and need for special education services, or the child and family are blamed for the behaviors. Parent advocacy groups and national mental health organizations need to increase awareness and services while changing perceptions of childhood psychiatric differences.

PROBLEMS ACCESSING MENTAL HEALTH RESOURCES

Problems also exist with the provision of mental health services for children who need them. Schools, with enactment of new state guidelines on reporting bullying, are currently reporting and addressing incidences of bullying behavior and applying behavioral analytic principles to them, however are not fiscally able to provide the necessary psychiatric treatments. Additionally, parents often deny their child's behavioral issues, are unwilling to access their health insurance, or have turned to available educational and mental health providers without effective resolution. Often challenged by parents, school response to students' mental health issues is dismal or reactive at best. Due to financial constraints resulting in not enough school psychologists, social workers, and guidance counselors, large caseloads result in not enough time to provide the school-based counseling needed. Even for special education students identified with emotional disorders, school psychological services are often limited, with minimal articulation between school personnel and private mental health providers. Furthermore, parents are often unaware of supports available, or neglect seeking them out due to the stigma of mental health issues.

TEACHER NAIVETÉ, DENIAL, AND LACK OF TRAINING

Bullying persists because some educators are either naïve or unwilling to get involved. Often, preschool teachers are not prepared to identify bullying behavior, are totally unaware of risk factors and possible mental health problems, and therefore unable to deliver appropriate interventions. Schools have codes of conduct and state mandates to report incidences of violence, anti-bullying requirements involving staff training, improved reporting mechanisms, workshops for new teachers and staff on discrimination, harassment, and bullying, however these programs are not mandated for teachers of preschool where bullying behaviors are developing. Schools do not sufficiently train teachers to understand risk factors for bullying behaviors as part of a preventative process. Educators need to understand that "the success of bullies in attaining resources and recognition—indeed, the very extent to which children turn to bullying—depends on factors that include the characteristics of the bully, the relationship existing between bullies and whom they target for harassment, and the reactions of classmates who witness bullying. Do schoolmates embarrass the harassed and stroke the bully's ego, do they ignore the bullying in front of their eyes, or does somebody intervene to support the victim and help stop the bullying?" "The importance of how peers and adults act in response to—or even better, in anticipation of bullying, can't be overestimated" (Rodkin, 2015, 5–6).

Children may have underlying psychiatric conditions that warrant more intense early intervening therapy in order to reduce aggression and susceptibility to personality disorder in adulthood. Research indicates great heterogeneity among children who bully, however children who bully often have superior self-esteem, lack of psychological stress, and enjoy social prestige among their classmates. Teacher training on common psychiatric disorders of childhood is needed because research shows bullying to be more frequent in children with emotional and conduct disorders. Teachers and support staff do not understand the nuances of bullying behavior, or how to differentiate between innocuous, infrequent teasing and persistent, chronic bullying. Preservice teachers are found to have limited post-secondary education preparing them to deal with bullying in school and differ in their perception of what actually constitutes bullying (Craig, Bell and Leschied 2011).

INEFFECTIVE PRACTICES: SUSPENSION, EXPULSION, AND PEER MEDIATION

Rather than developing proactive restorative policies, schools still use zero-tolerance policies including suspension and expulsion that are proven ineffective and get students into deeper trouble today compared to years past (Irby 2013). Skiba and Petersen (2000) found "little evidence supporting the effectiveness of suspension and expulsion for improving student behavior and school safety," especially for students most often targeted for disciplinary consequences with "suspension predicting further suspension, then eventually school dropout (35)." Suspension and expulsion serve to "accelerate the course of delinquency," putting students out on the street. In many cases, students who bully and are suspended often return to school engaging in bullying all over again, or transfer to a different one, with no change in behavior. Research suggests nonpunitive disciplinary methods result in bully and victimization reductions (Ttofi and Farrington 2011).

Aronson (2000) claims politically expedient, quick fix solutions such as clamping down on violence in the media, more stringent gun control, identifying students acting differently and removing them from school, are ineffective quick fixes. Schools should not allow bullying, taunting and insulting behavior and verbal violence much the same way workplaces do not allow the behavior in adults. As schools adopt early intervening efforts to effect behavioral change, the hope is that schools will replace suspension and expulsion with earlier, more efficacious interventions.

Research also demonstrates that use of peer mediation practices with students who bully is ineffective given their ability to manipulate others, actually providing an opportunity to exert influence and power. Ttofi and Farrington (2011) found peer mediation sessions may result in the escalation of behaviors of students who bully because they do not articulate being part of the problem and are not onboard to work toward a solution. Children who are victims often end up despondent, are bullied more after the meeting, then out of frustration, retaliate, and are suspended. Bullying persists because students who bully articulately deny their behaviors and administrators end up punishing the students who are victims.

PREVALENCE OF BULLYING OUTSIDE OF SCHOOL

School administrators and teachers are well aware of the impact family and community factors have on bully perpetration occurring outside of school. Turner et al. (2011) studying type and location of peer victimization in a national sample of children found a significant amount of peer victimization occurring outside of the school context. Children often model or react to behaviors of parents at home and then display them in school. Espelage, Low, Rao, Hong and Little (2014), studying violence and bullying, found that bullying and fighting perpetration mediated the link between family violence and substance use only in males, but not in females. Duncan (2011) found that bullies typically come from families with low cohesion, little warmth, absent fathers, high power needs, permit aggressive behavior, physical abuse, poor family functioning, and authoritarian parenting.

Exclusively focusing on school factors in the development of anti-bullying initiatives essentially ignores half the problem.

POOR APPLICATION OF RESEARCH TO PRACTICE

Bullying persists because of the lack of communication and collaboration among researchers, parents, school administrators, and teachers. "Academic isolation" or "elitism" of researchers leaves parents without practical solutions while practitioners develop curriculum and programs to prevent bullying without consulting the scholarly research on peer victimization, aggression, and bullying (Espelage 2012. In Goldman, C. 2012, Foreward). Clauses in teachers' contracts requiring educators to consult empirical research in developing curricula and programs are nonexistent and few mechanisms exist allowing for practitioner researcher collaboration. Academic social media websites are beginning to contribute to the dialogue, but the free flow of research between researcher and practitioner needs to improve in order to change the troubling landscape of school bullying.

SCHOLARLY RESEARCH LACKING

Clinical trials are difficult to conduct in classrooms because educational researchers rarely have access to experimental and control groups of students due to school superintendents' concerns for student privacy, fears of litigation and not knowing how to handle the evidence produced. Additionally there are ethical concerns of withholding intervention from groups of students needing them. Most studies often use indirect reporting of bullying through parental, teacher or student surveys where accuracy is questionable, because parents are not present, teachers often miss the bullying event, and children who bully deny it. It is clear that a new paradigm is needed where empirical research can be conducted in schools, considering broad parental consent, superintendents acting as Institutional Review Boards (IRB's), and results driving preventative efforts.

POOR DEFINITION OF RESPONSIBILITY AND
LIMITED RESOURCES IN SCHOOLS

Historically responsibilities of parents, schools systems, and mental health agencies have not been well defined when dealing with a student with chronic bullying behaviors. Parents sometimes take matters into their own hands causing conflict between families, resulting in the involvement of principals and superintendents to resolve the problem. Schools also have limited resources in dealing with the complexities of bullying. Tiers of support with increasing layers of interventions such as RtI are being effectively used to deal with behaviors in many schools, however schools rarely have the resources or personnel to deliver the intensive, long-term, therapeutic, one-to-one treatment the child who bullies needs. Although mandated by new state laws, tertiary interventions for children who persistently bully are loosely defined. Schools persist with attitudes such as "we just do not provide that type of counseling" because it the parents' fault, and a family issue, with family counseling outside the purview of schools. Unfortunately, with this attitude persisting, it perpetuates bullying and also contributes to the 50% of lifetime cases of mental illness beginning by age 14, with 20% of teens in the United States predicted to have a mental disorder at some point, with only about 36% receiving help (National Institute of Mental Health 2011).

INTERVENTIONS PROVIDED LATE

Furthermore, interventions are not timely, with aggressive behavior during preschool, kindergarten, and 1st grade often ignored and considered age-appropriate. Bullying needs to be recognized as a severe behavior that warrants remediation, especially during the early childhood years when behavioral change may be effective. Studies show children, when young, are more susceptible to parental and teacher influences, and initiatives designed for primary schools show more positive results than those aimed at adolescents (Bradshaw, Sawyer, and O'Brennan 2007).

SCHOOL ADMINISTRATOR CONSTRAINTS OF THE LAW

Problems also exist with the systems of support and constraints of educational laws. Principals, in charge of promoting a safe and tolerant school climate, often miss or ignore subtle bullying, especially when demonstrated by a popular student or athlete. Additionally, school administrators are often intimidated by aggressive, litigious and politically connected parents who may have a powerful presence in the community. Parents of children who bully sometimes display bullying behaviors as well, especially when defending their child. Additionally, although principals are required to report violence and bullying in their schools, they often underreport incidences to avoid their school being labeled violent and dangerous. Reluctance to report incidences to local law enforcement agencies also occurs because they do not want media attention to tarnish the district's reputation. As a result, incidences are reported late or not at all and bully perpetration continues, often by the same student from year to year.

EMOTIONALLY REACTIVE PARENTS AND DIFFICULTIES WITH BEHAVIOR MANAGEMENT

Parents frequently become emotionally reactive when educators criticize their child's bullying behaviors (Crothers and Kolbert 2008) and are accusatory rather than collaborative. Particularly challenging for educators are parents who do not make themselves available to meet with school personnel, do not create homes where respect is modeled, and do not acknowledge the bullying behaviors of their children. Parents, when informed of their child's bullying behavior on the bus or in school commonly deny the behavior or respond, "Why do you keep calling me?" "Why don't you just let kids be kids?" "What's the big deal?"

The problem is some parents have children with difficult behaviors, and other parents have children with appropriate behaviors that they cannot manage. Anyone who has been a parent knows how difficult it is to set limits with children and to be consistent with the consequences. Society has no mechanism by which parents receive behavioral training for children. Many parents have had poor role models themselves and have no idea of basic principles of behavior management. Parents customarily give their power away during the early years and then have difficulty managing their child's behavior as toddlers, and then during elementary and secondary school years. Children need limits to feel secure—they need their parents to parent, to be in charge, offering them the security of boundaries and structure. Parents need to get their power back (Today Show).

POOR ARTICULATION BETWEEN EDUCATORS FROM YEAR TO YEAR

Experience in educational settings has shown that communication among teachers is usually poor from year to year, especially in high schools due to the departmentalization of classes. Articulation meetings where behavioral data and effective interventions are shared from one year to the next are important to identify students who chronically bully peers. Students who bully are provided with a new venue each year where they can exercise their bullying prowess. Use of technology to track educational and behavioral progress could improve this situation.

LACK OF SUPERVISION IN UNSTRUCTURED SETTINGS

Schools do not adequately train school support personnel who are frequently responsible for children's safety during times when bullying is most frequent. School locker rooms, hallways, stairwells, playgrounds, cafeterias, and the bus are opportune venues for bullying to occur. School leaders frequently put their most untrained staff in the most unstructured school environments, leaving students who are unable to defend themselves as perfect targets (Heinrichs 2003). Bus drivers, lunch monitors, and recess personnel, often not privy to behavioral reports or the student's individualized educational program (IEP), do not know either the victim or the victimizer. One teacher shares a story:

> One year I had a student who was bullied by another student from a general education class. The bullying took place during lunch/recess when most bullies target their victims. Every day at lunch the student would bully my student for the way he spoke. The young boy had a stuttering problem and it would take him a long time to get his thoughts out. Many of the other students from the general education class would then make fun of him calling him names and pointing and laughing at him. Also, when I am on bus duty I have noticed that the bus is another time when bullies target their victims. There have been several instances when I have had to go onto the bus to talk to the students. It is always sad because the students with special needs cannot control or help how they act. Many students don't realize that and instead they bully them and make them feel more out of place. I have been a teacher for the past seven years. Every year I have noticed that bullying has become more and more of a problem. It always seems to get worse with each new school year. I find this especially occurs with the oldest students in the building.

PERSISTENCE OF BULLYING IN PHYSICAL EDUCATION CLASSES

Physical education classes are generally large with low teacher to student ratios, coupled with completely unsupervised locker rooms where students change their clothing and shower. Because of their tremendous vulnerability it is not surprising that students will often stay home from school on physical education days, and fail the class rather than be subjected to relentless victimization. O'Connor and Graber (2014) conducting a study on perceptions of teachers and 6th grade students about bullying in physical education class found adults to support bullying by providing mixed information regarding social interactions while ignoring the non-physical acts of bullying. Appearance, body size, physical ability and personal attire contributed to more bullying while student's fears prevented them from reporting bullying and assisting victims. Unsafe feelings impact a student's desire to participate. Peer harassment still existing in physical education environments contributes to a culture of bullying and fear.

School leaders as change agents need to replace ineffective practices and adopt new ways to deal with bullying in schools.

Chapter 2

The Hostile Environment

Legal Aspects of School Bullying

Between 1990 and 2010, more than 120 bills were enacted by state legislatures addressing bullying, and now disciplinary policies are required in three-fourths of states, but law and policy about bullying remains fragmented and inconsistent (Cornell and Limber 2015). Although consequences for students engaging in bullying are mandated, suspension, expulsion, and zero-tolerance policies are unsupported empirically (American Psychological Association Zero Tolerance Task Force 2008). One-third of state laws require the provision of counseling for students who bullied and are victimized, but are unclear on its delivery. Bullying reported by the media evokes a harsh and emotional societal response. Similar to the disjoint between research and practice, there exists a division between law and practice, where educators are often unaware of the legal ramifications of bullying. Theoretically, educators who understand federal and state laws and repercussions of failing to comply may be more motivated to consistently report bullying behaviors among students and utilize preventions with fidelity. As States tighten educator certification and professional development requirements to include bullying workshops and improve reporting practices in schools, now is the opportune time to conduct studies on effects of these initiatives on the reduction of bullying.

STATES' ANTI-BULLYING, DISCRIMINATION, AND HARASSMENT LAWS

Fifty state legislatures have enacted anti-bullying laws many named for students who took their lives. Montana was the last state in the nation to do so, taking 10 years to enact its anti-bullying law. Democratic Governor Steve

Bullock signed the Bully Free Montana Act at Jefferson Elementary School in Helena in April 2015 (Baumann, 2015).

Suicides of youth have had a strong impact on schools and significantly influenced anti-bullying initiatives. Although it is unlikely that traditional and cyberbullying *by themselves* leads to youth suicide it tends to exacerbate already present emotional challenges that students may have (Hinduja and Patchin 2009). The following laws are named after the students who took their lives.

- Vermont: (Ryan Halligan)
- Missouri: Megan Meier (Megan Meier CyberBullying Prevention Act)
- Ohio: Jessica Logan (Jessica Logan Act)
- New Jersey: Tyler Clementi
- Florida: Jeffrey Johnson (Jeffrey Johnson Stand Up for All Students Act)
- Idaho: Jared High (Jared's Law)
- Kansas: Loren Wendelburg (Loren's Law)
- Maryland: Grace McComas (Grace's Law)
- Massachusetts: Phoebe Prince
- California: Seth Walsh (Seth's Law)
- Oklahoma: April Himes

Stronger state anti-bullying laws have resulted in schools expanding existing codes of conduct to include language with clear definitions of harassment and bullying, processes for identifying and reporting it, and consequences for those involved. State laws vary in scope and many are unfunded. Massachusetts, known for its strong anti-bullying laws defines school bullying:

> Bullying is the repeated use by one or more students or by a member of a school staff including, but not limited to, an educator, administrator, school nurse, cafeteria worker, custodian, bus driver, athletic coach, advisor to an extracurricular activity or paraprofessional of a written, verbal or electronic expression or a physical act or gesture or any combination thereof, directed at a victim that: (i) causes physical or emotional harm to the victim or damage to the victim's property; (ii) places the victim in reasonable fear of harm to himself or damage to his property; (iii) creates a hostile environment at school for the victim; (iv) infringes on the rights of the victim at school; or (v) materially and substantially disrupts the education process or the orderly operation of a school. For the purposes of this section, bullying shall include cyber-bullying (Massachusetts Department of Education).

New York State also amended education law (New York Education Department Sec. 801 Law SS10-18) to include tolerance, respect for others, and dignity. Under the New York State Dignity for All Students Act (DASA) (New York State Education Department, 2012), harassment and discrimination of individuals on school property or at school functions based on a person's actual or perceived race, color, weight, national origin, ethnic group, religion, religious practice, disability, sexual orientation, gender identity, or sex is prohibited. Interestingly, the protected category of weight was added to DASA last. Bullying based on weight has persisted through history and permeates society.

School districts in New York are mandated to thoroughly train a staff member to handle sensitive issues of harassment and discrimination and as of January 1, 2014, all newly certifying teachers must complete six hours of training on bullying, harassment and discrimination (Chapter 102 of the Laws of 2012). School principals are required to report incidences concerning school safety and the education climate disaggregated by race, ethnicity, and other populations. Districts are also required to report information to the public in a manner that complies with student privacy rights under the Family Educational Rights and Privacy Act (20 U.S.C. 1232).

Anti-discrimination and harassment law under school codes of conduct have been in effect for years, along with requirements that school districts report data on incidences of violence to their state education departments. Currently, it is now recognized that student bullying specifically falling under school anti-bullying policies, may also trigger responsibilities under one or more of the anti-discrimination statutes enforced by the United States Department of Education Office of Civil Rights (OCR). Specifically,

> Bullying occurring in schools often reaches the level of discrimination and harassment when it is based on a student's race, color, national origin, sex or disability and is sufficiently serious causing a hostile environment, and where school employees encourage, tolerate, do not adequately address, or ignore the harassment, a student's civil rights are infringed upon (United States Commission on Civil Rights 2011).

Schools in violation of students' federal civil rights are at risk of losing Federal funds and paying damages to the injured party if bullying constitutes harassment under the following federal laws:

1. Title VI of the Civil Rights Act of 1964 protecting discrimination based on race, color, or national origin (Title VI, Pub. L 88-352, 78 Stat. 241)
2. Title IX of the Education Amendments of 1972 (Title IX, 20 U.S.C. 1681a) on the basis of sex
3. Section 504 of the Rehabilitation Act of 1973 (29 U.S.C. Sec. 794)

4. Title II of the Americans with Disabilities Act of 1990 (Title II, 42 U.S.C. Sections 12101-12213)
5. Individuals with Disabilities Education Act of 2004 (20 U.S.C. 1400).

School attorneys customarily assist school boards of education in developing appropriate codes of conduct including the new State anti-bullying and existing federal civil right laws.

DELIBERATE INDIFFERENCE AND SUBSTANTIAL DISRUPTION

The deliberate indifference standard resulting from The Davis v. Monroe County Board of Education (1999) case determined peer on peer harassment results in liability to the school district when the harassment creates a hostile environment with consequences for the involved student including deprivation of educational opportunity. In the Davis case, a female student was sexually harassed, resulting in her grades dropping and the contemplation of suicide. The school informed of the harassment and doing nothing to stop it, was found to be deliberately indifferent. Schools across the United States are now responsible to act quickly in response to acts of bullying and if they know or reasonably should know of possible student-on-student harassment, immediately take steps to end the harassment, eliminate the hostile environment, and prevent its recurrence (University of the State of New York 2010).

Much of the existing litigation is responsive to schools demonstrating deliberate indifference when failing to investigate incidences of bullying. Schools can be held liable if they are indifferent to parental concerns or attempt to suppress the problem. Minimizing bullying incidences may require school districts to pay monetary damages to the injured party, pay for private tutoring or compensatory services, and result in losing Federal funds. Schools by law are required to not only discipline the child who bullies, but eliminate the hostile environment caused by it, address its effects and take steps to ensure that it does not reoccur (Maag and Katisyannis 2012). Unfortunately, current practices of suspending students who perpetrate bullying have only short-term consequences because frequently they return to school after the suspension to resume bullying, contributing to the hostile environment.

Rulings from other cases apply to bullying in schools such as the 1969 Supreme Court case *Tinker v. Des Moines Independent Community School District*, allowing discipline of students for speech outside of school only if it causes a "material and substantial disruption" in school. The substantial disruption clause is frequently used in litigation where students' free speech is challenged. Schools have to interpret whether cyberbullying for example, occurring outside school is considered free speech and whether it has caused a substantial disruption in school.

RESEARCH ON CASE LAW

Case law on school bullying has exploded in recent years. Searching Google Scholar and Case Law, a multitude of cases appeared: McGlothlin v. Iowa (March 11, 2015), Diperna v. Chicago School of Professional Psychology, Lamberth, Lamberth, et al. v. Clark County School District, Nevada (July 1, 2015), Wilder v. Milwaukee Public Schools System, (June 16, 2015), Donoho v. County of Sonoma (June 22, 2015), and Peterson v. Kramer, Superintendent Northeastern Local School District (April 29, 2015). Holben and Zirkel (2014) systematically analyzed case law related to student bullying in public schools from 1992 through 2011, finding evidence of a steady growth in bullying cases. They looked specifically at characteristics of the plaintiff and defendants, type of rulings in terms of possible violations of The Equal Protection Clause of the Fourteenth Amendment, Title IX, negligence laws, trends in frequencies of rulings, and outcomes. They also examined if rulings were in favor of the plaintiffs (the student or the student's parents) or the defendants (school district or employees) overall and over time. Using Olweus' definition of bullying, there were 166 court decisions with 84% of the plaintiffs being members of a protected class including gender (n=67), disability (n=27), perceived sexual orientation (n=25), and race/ethnicity (n=25). Defendants (n=163) included types of institutions such as school districts and school boards. The most frequent legal basis for the rulings revolved around Title IX, Fourteenth Amendment due process, and Fourteenth Amendment equal protection laws with claim rulings in favor of the defendants (62%) and plaintiffs (2%). Significantly more rulings for the defendants demonstrates the strong need to educate teachers about bullying, especially when it rises to the level of harassment and discrimination.

STUDENTS WITH DISABILITIES WHO ARE BULLIED: LEGAL RAMIFICATIONS

Students with disabilities are bullied significantly more than any other population of students. Under the Individuals with Disabilities Education Act (IDEA, 2004) students with disabilities have rights to a Free Appropriate Public Education (FAPE). Public schools are mandated to provide instruction designed to meet the unique needs of students with disabilities and education reasonably calculated to confer education benefit resulting in progress toward their goals (Board of Education of the Hendrick Hudson Central School District v. Rowley, 1982). Legal counsel is now advising many districts across the country that common practices involving students with disabilities are a denial of FAPE:

- Families, desperate for the safety and welfare of their child with a disability, as a result of the district's inability to end the bullying, will move in order that their child can attend school safely in another district.
- The student with a disability fears going to school because of being bullied.
- The student is placed in a class that may be more (protective) but does not meet their academic needs or is assigned a 1-1 aide (for their protection) resulting in the denial of FAPE in the least restrictive environment (LRE). (U. S. Department of Education 2013).

Bullying of a student with a disability could constitute a form of discrimination, and disability harassment under Section 504 and Title II. Districts must identify whether a reported incident amounts to unlawful discrimination and if so, respond in a manner consistent with Section 504 (Weatherly, 34). A student who incessantly taunts or ridicules a student with a disability, hits him with things on the bus, throws his personal items out the window, or takes his lunch, may result in the student not attending school. When those who are bullying fail to stop despite district efforts, this may constitute disability harassment and the failure of the school to meet obligations under Section 504 and Title II (Office of Special Education and Research 2013, 9). The district is obligated to discipline the offending students and eliminate the hostile environment. Schools must consult with the district's Section 504 or Title II coordinator, train staff on recognizing and responding to harassment of students with disabilities, and monitor the situation to ensure that harassment does not resume.

STUDENTS WITH DISABILITIES WHO
BULLY: LEGAL RAMIFICATIONS

Kaukiainen et al. (2002) found that students with high-incidence disabilities such as learning disabilities and ED perpetrate bullying twice as often as students without. Cho, Hendrickson, and Mock (2009) found 60% of students with disabilities to be identified as bullies, victims, or bully-victims. The student who bullies may be a student with a disability having an emotional or behavior disorder having unique protections under the IDEA.

The Honig v. Doe case (1988) set the legal standard for suspending students with disabilities for up to ten school days when they pose an immediate threat to the safety of others. Current IDEA law (2004) states a student classified with ED for example, suspended for bullying, may be considered for a change of placement. Certain procedures need to be followed when a change of placement would be a removal of the current educational placement generally for more than ten days in a school year. There must be a manifestation determination meeting called to determine if the conduct in question was caused by, or had a direct and substantial relationship to, the child's disability or the direct result of the local educational agency's failure to implement the IEP. If the parents and the members of the IEP team determine the conduct is related to the student's disability the team must conduct a functional behavior assessment and develop a behavioral intervention plan (BIP), review or modify an existing behavior intervention plan, and return the student to the placement from which he/she was removed, unless the parent and the school district agree to a change of placement as part of modification of the BIP. Under the IDEA's 45-day special circumstance rule, school personnel may remove a student to an interim alternative education setting without regard to whether the behavior is a manifestation of the student's disability when the student carries or possesses a weapon to school, possesses or uses illegal drugs, or inflicts serious bodily injury on another person.

The IEP team must determine what services are to be provided for any removal period beyond ten days in a school year, in order to continue to participate in the general curriculum and work on achieving IEP goals. Schools' in-school suspension (ISS) is not considered a part of the days of suspension toward a change in placement "as long as the child is afforded the opportunity to continue to appropriately participate in the general curriculum, continue to receive the services specified on the child's IEP and continue to participate with nondisabled children to the extent they would have in their current placement" (Weatherly, 27).

A bus suspension also must be treated as a disciplinary removal and all of the IDEA's discipline procedures applicable to children with disabilities apply if it is listed on the IEP. If a student is suspended from transportation for more than 20 consecutive schools days, that suspension constitutes a change of placement and this triggers the requirement for a manifestation determination meeting.

CHILD-FIND REQUIREMENTS OF IDEA AND BULLY PERPETRATION

School districts, under the child-find provision of IDEA are also required to initiate the special education referral process when they suspect a child has a disability. This has important implications for children persistently and chronically bullying others, because they may meet the criteria of having an emotional disability, necessitating referral to special education for initial evaluation. Milwaukee Public Schools lost a case when it failed to refer children with suspected disabilities in a timely manner for initial evaluations, imposing suspensions that improperly impeded its ability to refer children with suspected disabilities for an initial evaluation. As part of the settlement, the defendants were required to refer 95% of students in kindergarten -5th grade who were suspended ten or more days during a school year and 95% of students in grades 6–12 suspended 20 or more days in a school year to a system of early intervening services designed to address behavioral issues that resulted in suspensions and consider an evaluation referral to determine special education eligibility (Gamm 2009, 24–5). This case illustrates the intent of the court, (i.e., to proactively provide needed early intervention then consider referral to special education to determine if the child has a disability).

Typically, districts must conduct an evaluation within 60 days. Students found to have an emotional disability have rights to FAPE with an IEP to meet their unique needs, often involving counseling and special programming.

IDEA REFERENCES TO BEHAVIOR APPLYING TO BULLY PERPETRATION

The student with an emotional disability who bullies needs interventions to address the behavior. Under IDEA, when the behavior of a child with a disability impedes the child's learning or the learning of others, the IEP team must consider "the use of positive behavioral interventions and supports, and other strategies, to address that behavior" (Gamm, 2009, 52). School IEP teams must assess a student in all areas of suspected disability. There are times when a psychiatric evaluation is necessary and parents are asked to have their child evaluated under their medical insurance. If the parent refuses, the district is not relieved of its responsibilities to evaluate the student in all areas of suspected need including a psychiatric evaluation. While school personnel should refrain from diagnosing medical or psychiatric conditions or suggesting medication, information from reports is always shared and considered at IEP meetings in order to determine special education eligibility and programming. School officials may provide input at parents' request and with their consent about a student's behavior, may aid medical professionals in making the diagnosis (Weatherly, 5).

Additionally, the 2004 IDEA Amendments prohibit State and district personnel from requiring the child to obtain a prescription for a substance covered by the Controlled Substances Act as a condition of attending school, receiving an evaluation or receiving services.

STUDENTS IDENTIFYING AS LESBIAN, GAY, BISEXUAL, OR TRANSGENDERED (LGBT): LEGAL RAMIFICATIONS

Students identifying as LGBT are also bullied at significantly higher rates, but are not a protected class under federal law. The proposed bill, The Student Non-Discrimination Act of 2011 has not been passed at this time, however protections exist under many state laws. According to the Gay, Lesbian and Straight Education Network (GLSEN 2009), 84.6% of LGBT youth were verbally harassed, 40.1% physically harassed, 18.8% physically assaulted, and 52.9% cyberbullied at school in the previous year because of their sexual orientation.

One case in particular influenced law across the United States. The Nabozny v. Podlesny case (1996) involved 19-year-old Jamie Nabozny who sued his school district and administrators from his middle and high schools for neglecting to protect him from incessant bullying and harassment based on his gender and sexual orientation. Mrs. Podlesny, a school administrator remarked that "boys will be boys," and that "if Jamie was going to act so openly gay he had to expect this stuff to happen to him" (Teaching tolerance.org). The district lost and paid the plaintiff damages in the amount of $900,000, because the court found that the defendants would have protected him from harassment from peers had he not been gay, violating his U.S. Constitution 14th Amendment rights to equal protection. Courts are frequently hearing cases questioning a school's alleged negligence in failing to stop the bullying of a student leading to their suicide (Wolfson 2015).

There is a shift toward criminalizing bullying (Cascardi et al. 2014) where assault, battery, extortion, robbery, stalking, or threatening may be involved. Concerns exist because the concept of bullying may be too broad and subjective for reasonable application in the criminal justice system. Can schools determine that bullying constitutes a criminal offense? The Iowa Supreme Court holds that evidence of taunting is insufficient to constitute criminal harassment (D.S. 856 N.W. 2d 348 Iowa 2014). In this particular case, a fifteen-year-old female (D.S.) was charged with harassing her classmate, calling her "T bitch." Another female (T.B.) thought she was addressing her when D.S. responded, "I wasn't talking to you, you fat skanky bitch!" After being reported to the police, the juvenile court found that D.S. committed a delinquent act because she threatened, intimidated, and alarmed her peer as required by Iowa's criminal harassment statutes. D.S. was substantially shorter and weighed less than T.B. and thus, the court found it was not reasonable to assume she anticipated any threat of physical harm, only intimidation, thus committing a delinquent act (May 2015). The court then reversed this decision finding that "intimidation" must be restricted to true threat with the intent of placing the victim in fear of bodily harm or death. Additionally, D.S. had not initiated any "purposeful personal contact" with the victim. This case implies that criminalizing bullying is up for debate and may depend on the nature of its initiation and intent. The court additionally had concerns that verbal intimidation may be considered free speech. Evidence of taunting alone is insufficient to constitute criminal harassment (Harvard Law Review 128, 2058).

CONCLUSION

Research needs to explore the effects of litigation and legislation in changing bullying with the enactment of new state anti-bullying laws. Also, research is needed to determine whether teachers, parents, and students are sufficiently aware of federal and state anti-bullying, harassment and discrimination laws, and whether knowledge of these laws is having the intended effect of reducing and eliminating bullying and harassment. Meyer and Stader (2009) argue schools need to educate teachers and principals on their legal and professional responsibilities in working with LGBT youth. Training on legal and professional responsibilities for all students needs to be proactive and include *parents* and the community. Holben and Zirkel (2014) argue lack of funding and confusion of anti-bullying laws suggests that enforcement of bullying rests on the expertise of K-12 schools to determine best practices to garner respect and dignity for all students. Anti-bullying laws need to be applied consistently in schools, with teachers and support personnel receiving training annually to review implications of federal and state laws especially dealing with the impact of indifference to bullying.

State anti-bullying legislation and enhanced schools' codes of conduct are many years overdue. As a society, we should be ashamed, appalled, and disappointed by our inability to protect vulnerable children, including children who perpetrate and children who are targeted. Other initiatives have displaced emphasis on social justice and the health and safety of our children.

Chapter 3

Characteristics, Correlates and Risk Factors of Bully Perpetrators

Anti-bullying programs have increased the awareness of the bullying problem but many educators are still unprepared to intervene. While physical, face-to-face bullying is easily identifiable, most types of bullying involve covert, manipulative, behaviors with the bully perpetrators motivated by desires to be at the top of their peer group targeting those who are not able to defend themselves. Through subtle taunting sometimes carried out by others, children who bully use dominance to elevate their peer status by marginalizing weaker children. Often students are suspended instead of being provided with appropriate interventions for the behavior, resulting in the continuation of bullying upon returning to school.

What is the science behind aggressive bullying behavior? Is bullying the early manifestation of conduct disorders (CD) and antisocial personality disorders and is remediation possible? Can educators successfully change the behavior of the child who bullies, and will this involve long-term and intensive therapy? What specific types of strategies work? Do these treatments have efficacy even for the older adolescent or are efforts to remediate futile? Is there more of a biological basis for behavior where some of us are born with traits of aggression and the need to dominate? Goodall, an ethnologist working with chimpanzees since 1960, made major discoveries in personality and individual traits between dominant male chimps, describing Frodo who even as a child bullied the other young chimps. "Very often, if two were playing and saw Frodo come along, they stopped playing because they knew as soon as he joined in, he'd hurt one of them" (Quammen 2014, 56). Are some children actually resistant to change and unable to learn empathy? What does the research base provide in examining the child who persistently creates a hostile environment in school?

Forness (2003) suggests looking at bullying from a developmental psychopathology approach, where knowledge of psychological and behavioral dysfunctions occurring in mental disorders is used to improve their early identification and prevention. Generally, teacher candidates receive only several courses on psychiatric comorbidity and psychopharmacology as they apply to school behavioral intervention, and although special and general educators do not make medical or pharmacological suggestions for students, it is important that higher education programs include coursework in these areas. This in turn should help teachers understand and increase prospects of accurate identification and utilization of appropriate interventions for populations of increasingly psychiatrically challenged youth. Application of this approach may also be effective in reducing bullying behaviors among students.

WHY CONSIDER RISK FACTORS OF BULLYING?

Exploring the available research among related disciplines can assist with identifying possible correlates and risk factors of bullying behaviors in children, and increase educators' understanding of frequently occurring psychiatric and emotional conditions comorbid with bullying. Exploring the research can offer different perspectives leading to the implementation of appropriate research-based interventions in schools. Because educators do not understand how bullying presents, tighter school anti-bullying laws may not have the intended effect of reducing school bullying. Schools need to adopt a new framework where children who bully *and* their families are provided with the intensity of behavioral interventions and supports needed.

POOR OUTCOMES: ASSOCIATION WITH CRIMINALITY LATER IN LIFE

Bullying is recognized internationally as a complex event with severe consequences for children who bully later in life. "Rarely does any single behavior predict future problems as clearly as bullying does . . . ." (Kumpulainen 2008, 121). Olweus (1998) studying bullying behaviors of one thousand 6th, 7th, and 8th grade boys found their aggressive behaviors to be stable over time, even with environmental changes, especially if they had reached eight or nine years old. Approximately 5% of the males sampled were aggressive physically and verbally against peers where teachers had a positive attitude toward violence, had average popularity, were tough, confident, and had average to below average academic achievement.

Sourander et al. (2007, 402) found that children who bullied and presented with psychiatric symptoms at age eight were at significant risk of antisocial personality disorder as young adults. Seventy percent of students who bullied ended up engaging in criminal behavior in adulthood. Vaughn, et al. (2011) examining the psychiatric and behavioral characteristics of 43,000 individuals from the United States over 18 years of age, found approximately 5% of respondents were involved in forms of antisocial and externalizing behaviors with extensive psychiatric disturbance. Educators should be aware that, "there may be a child in every classroom who is part of this 5% subset" (79). Because psychiatric characteristics in youth persist into adulthood (Vaughn et al. 2010) and those who bully are 11 times more likely to have a CD and eight times more likely to meet criteria for antisocial personality disorder, a stronger system of prevention needs to be put in place for this 5% subset (192).

INDIVIDUALS WITH DISABILITIES EDUCATION ACT (IDEA): SOCIAL EMOTIONAL AND EMOTIONAL DISABILITY CLASSIFICATION

Schools have responsibilities under the IDEA of 2004 to identify and provide special education services for those identified with emotional disturbance impacting educational performance. Under the regulations:

Emotional Disturbance means a condition exhibiting one or more of the following characteristics over a long period of time and to a marked degree that adversely affects a child's educational performance:

a. An inability to learn that cannot be explained by intellectual, sensory, or health factors.
b. An inability to build or maintain satisfactory interpersonal relationships with peers and teachers.
c. Inappropriate types of behavior or feelings under normal circumstances.
d. A general pervasive mood of unhappiness or depression.
e. A tendency to develop physical symptoms or fears associated with personal or school problems.
f. Emotional disturbance includes schizophrenia. The term does not apply to children who are socially maladjusted, unless it is determined that they have an emotional disturbance under paragraph (c)(4)(i) of this section. (IDEA, 2004).

Children with emotional disturbance or emotional disorders (ED) may also have underlying psychiatric disorders that significantly interfere with learning. Special education assessment needs to include psychiatric evaluation early in the process of identifying a student's eligibility for special education when the need is apparent.

A special education teacher shares,

> In my second year of teaching there was a student each staff member knew
> by his first name. He was briefly placed in my co-teaching classroom and then
> quickly removed because he began picking on the special education students.
> He was a bright boy who showed little patience for slower learners. He was a
> child who needed intense intervention. Through word of mouth, I heard that he
> was bipolar and on and off medications. His mother was an alcoholic, dad was
> not around, and his aunt was his main caregiver. The student walked around like
> he owned the school. Often times, it seemed like we let him. But I'll never forget
> the few times I saw him cry. I can't remember why he was crying anymore, but
> it stays with me as a cry for help. I truly hope he is doing well and has continu-
> ously received support from his educational team.

ASSUMPTION OF GOOD SELF-ESTEEM

Despite the prevalence of anti-bullying programs over the several decades,
many practicing teachers and administrators still hold the erroneous belief
that a child who bullies has poor self-esteem and as a result, strategies to
build self-worth are ineffective. The child who bullies generally has high self-
regard, feels good about what he does, and uses powerful techniques to boost
prestige among peers (Reijntjes et al. 2013). Examining bullying in youth
from late childhood into early adolescence, from the bully's perspective, the
benefits of bullying outweighed the costs. Children with high rates of bullying behavior were positively related to high social status, few internalizing
problems, and perceived social competence. Findings indicate that children
who bully continue because the costs and consequences to them are minimal
and not worth changing their behaviors. Interventions for children who bully
need to concentrate on alternative consequences that are more socially appropriate and important for them, where they can retain peer status and healthy
feelings of social competence.

Findings translate into the importance of identifying characteristics and
psychological traits seen in children who bully and providing specific training
to improve teachers' understanding.

MOTIVATING FACTORS

A woman leading an anti-bullying training session, shared she bullied as a
child because it made her feel good. Jacobson (2010) examined the phenomenon of bully perpetration from the perspective of children who bully and

found that some children admit they derive satisfaction from bullying peers and enjoy making their victim(s) cry. Perren et al. (2001) found that children who bully are more morally disengaged than noninvolved students and act as though their victims deserve the bullying (Kowalski and Witte 2006). They do not consider their behaviors inappropriate, have a high need for dominance and power (Graham and Juvonen 1998), and are adept at finding victims who pose no threat to them or their social status (Perry, Willard and Perry 1990). Children who bully are often rewarded for their behavior materially through money, other possessions taken from peers, or psychologically, through achieving high social status and prestige (Kowalski, Limber, and Agatston 2008). Research also suggests children who bully have dominant personalities and like to assert themselves with force; they have tempers, are impulsive, easily frustrated and have positive attitudes toward violence compared to other children. Camodeca and Goossens (2005) found that students who bully have difficulty following rules, appear tough, sometimes relate to adults in aggressive ways, and are good at talking themselves out of difficult situations. They engage in both proactive, deliberate aggression to achieve a goal, and reactive aggression, being defensive when provoked. They are often popular, with other students supportive of their bullying, and possess good skills at reading the mental states of others (Sutton, Smith, and Swettenham 1999). Researchers regard bullying as a complex event caused by many variables.

PERSISTENCE AND LONGEVITY OF BULLY PERPETRATION

Longitudinal studies demonstrate the persistence of childhood bullying and resistance of bully perpetrators to behavioral change. An analysis studying children at age eight and then again at 12 years old, measured the persistence of behaviors and the relationship between bullying and psychological disturbance. Of the 1268 Finnish children (Kumpulainen, Rasanen, and Henttonen 1999), males outnumbered females, and nearly half the children involved in bullying who bullied at eight were still bullying at 12, and had significantly more psychiatric symptoms at both points, including psychological disturbance compared to other children regardless of socioeconomic status. Nine years later, Kumpulainen (2008) found attention-deficit hyperactivity disorder (ADHD), depression, and anxiety to be risk correlates of bullying. Male victims had anxiety, male bullies, personality disorders, and male bully-victims had both personality disorders and anxiety in adulthood. Children who were disturbed when involved in bullying at school age were at greater risk. Juvonen, Graham, and Schuster (2003) found 22% of students involved in bullying were perpetrators (7%), victims (9%), or both (65%). Bully-victims were the most troubled, displaying the highest levels of conduct, school and peer relationship problems and were least engaged in school, depressed and lonely.

THE BULLY-VICTIM

Research consistently demonstrates children who engage in both bullying and victimization are at the greatest risk for developing multiple psycho-pathological behaviors compared to pure bullies (Kim, et al. 2006) and have the most severe negative outcomes. Wolke et al. (2013) found bully-victims to have the worst health outcomes in adulthood with an increased likelihood of being diagnosed with a serious illness, having been diagnosed with a psychiatric disorder, regular smoking, and slow recovery from illness while bully-victims were more likely to have ADHD, CD, or oppositional defiant disorder (ODD).

CHILDREN WHO BULLY AND POPULARITY

Children who bully are found to be psychologically strongest, popular, and enjoy high social standing, in contrast to victims who are emotionally dis-tressed, socially marginalized and display internalizing behaviors. They are powerful with leadership qualities, report feeling good about themselves and their peer interactions, and are viewed by peers as physically attractive, wear-ing stylish clothing and athletic (Vaillancourt, Hymel, and McDougall 2003). Book, Volk and Hosher (2012, 220), contrary to popular belief, found "bul-lies can engage in targeted aggression while still maintaining the capacity of supportive friendships." They have more leadership skills compared to nonin-volved children, belong to larger social clusters, and frequently affiliate with other bullies (Perren and Alsaher 2006). Children who bully are sometimes preferred playmates, particularly among other aggressive boys. Preschoolers socially dominant and socially prominent win positive peer regard where peers find power holders physically attractive even if they are aggressive (Hawley et al. 2007) This is confirmed by Undheim and Sund (2010), while finding bullies to have higher aggression and delinquency scores, have lower social problems scores and higher scores on the social acceptance scales com-pared to students who were bullied. On the contrary, however Dijkstra, Lin-denberg and Veenstra (2008), examining the extent that bullying behavior of popular adolescents had on peer acceptance and peer rejection found bullying behavior of popular students was associated with less peer acceptance and more peer rejection.

Students who bully generally may be popular and have high social status. Proactive response when popular students are the source of bullying may have significant effects on reducing overall school bullying rates. Despite aggressive behaviors displayed by popular and physically attractive children, teachers may resist responding to their aggressive acts, thus socially reinforcing the inappropriate behavior (Hawley et al. 2007).

Research on teacher's differential treatment of popular children who bully and are aggressive must continue.

ASSOCIATIONS BETWEEN BULLY PERPETRATION AND MENTAL HEALTH DISORDERS

Research demonstrates associations between bullying behaviors and CD, ODD, ADHD (Zablotsky et al. 2013), antisocial personality disorders, and depression (Kumpulainen 2008; Coolidge, DenBoer and Segal 2004). Students who continuously bully are predicted to have current and future psychiatric symptoms (Undheim and Sund 2010) and are susceptible to future problems of violence and delinquency (Ryan and Smith 2009). Benedict, Vivier and Gjelsvik (2014) found a diagnosis of depression, anxiety and ADHD that was strongly associated with being identified as a bully.

Males are found to have higher rates of aggressive behavior (Craig et al. 2009) and are at risk of personality disorders, with 24% of middle and high school students ending up in jail by age 25. Soulander et al. (2007), found that boys who frequently bullied were predicted to have antisocial personality disorders, a wide array of conduct and substance abuse problems, with high levels of depressive, aggressive, and delinquent behaviors. Of the sample, 28% of children identified at risk had a psychiatric disorder 10 to 15 years later. Yen et al. (2014) also found comorbid mental health problems among adolescents dependent on the level and types of bullying. Perpetrators of both passive bullying and active bullying were significantly associated with mental health problems, with passive bullies having general anxiety and active not. Perpetrators of both active and passive bullying had more severe depression and hyperactivity/impulsivity than perpetrators of only passive or only active types of bullying. Stellwagon and Keurig (2012) performing a study examining the association of ringleader bullying with psychopathic traits and theory of mind among 100 youth receiving inpatient psychiatric services found a relationship between bullying behavior and high levels of narcissism and social acuity.

Studies increasing associate bully perpetration with ADHD, updated in the fifth edition of the *Diagnostic and Statistical Manual of Mental Disorders* (APA 2013):

Characterized by a pattern of behavior, present in multiple settings (e.g., school and home), that can result in performance issues in social, educational, or work settings. As in DSM-IV, symptoms will be divided into two categories of inattention and hyperactivity and impulsivity that include behaviors like failure to pay close attention to details, difficulty organizing tasks and activities, excessive talking, fidgeting, or an inability to remain seated in appropriate situations. Children must have at least six symptoms from either (or both) the inattention group of criteria, the hyperactivity and impulsivity criteria, while older adolescents and adults (over age 17 years) must present with five. Using DSM-5, several of the individual's ADHD symptoms must be present prior to age 12 years, compared to 7 years as the age of onset in DSM-IV (APA 2013).

Ismail et al. (2014) exploring socio-demographic and psychological factors associated with bullying behavior among 12 year olds in Malaysian schools found risk factors for bullying included male gender, hyperactive and inattentive ADHD symptoms and conduct behavior. This study provides more evidence of the relationship between ADHD and possible association with CD. The authors theorized, "ADHD symptoms may be the contributing factor in bullying behavior initially, but the development of CD continues to perpetuate or worsen the bullying problem in adolescence" (S118). Findings suggest the benefits of early detection of ADHD and CD with early provision of counseling and behavioral change, with a focus less on punishment and more on intervention. Behaviors should be closely monitored by pediatricians through routine well-child screening coupled with schools using validated behavioral assessments available to prekindergarten teachers as part of the data collection process. Prekindergarten providers need training for familiarity with these instruments, regardless of administering them or not.

Research also suggests associations between bullying and ODD where the student:

Displays a pattern of negativistic, hostile and defiant behavior lasting at least six months, during which four (or more) of the following are present: 1) Often loses temper 2) Often argues with adults 3) Often actively defies or refuses to comply with adult's requests or rules 4) Often deliberately annoys people 5) Often blames others for his or her mistakes or misbehavior 6) Is often touchy or easily annoyed by others 7) Is often angry and resentful 8) Is often spiteful or vindictive (APA, 2000, 68).

Fite et al. (2014) performed a study to determine the relationship between symptoms of ADHD and ODD and bullying-victimization in adolescence. Findings indicated that ODD symptoms were more strongly associated with both bullying and victimization than ADHD symptoms, and the effects of ODD symptoms on physical forms of both bullying and victimization were stronger for males than females. Farrington and Baldry (2010) longitudinally studying 411 London males from ages eight to age forty-eight found the most important risk factors of bullying to be hyperactivity-impulsiveness and low empathy.

Studies also demonstrate bully perpetration to be associated with CD defined:

> CD is characterized by behavior that violates either the rights of others or major societal norms. At least 3 symptoms must be present in the past 12 months with one symptom having been present in the past 6 months. To be diagnosed with CD, the symptoms must cause significant impairment in social, academic, or occupational functioning. The disorder is typically diagnosed prior to adulthood (APA, 2013)

Specifically:

> Aggression to people and animals: 1) often bullies, threatens, or intimidates others 2) often initiates physical fights 3) has used a weapon that can cause serious physical harm to others (e.g., a bat, brick, broken bottle, knife, gun) 4) has been physically cruel to people 5) has been physically cruel to animals 6) has stolen while confronting a victim (e.g., mugging, purse snatching, extortion, armed robbery) 7) has forced someone into sexual activity. Destruction of Property: 8) has deliberately engaged in fire setting with the intention of causing serious damage 9) has deliberately destroyed others' property (other than by fire setting). Deceitfulness or theft: 10) has broken into someone else's house, building, or car (11) often lies to obtain goods or favors or to avoid obligations (i.e., "cons" others) 12) has stolen items of nontrivial value without confronting a victim (e.g., shoplifting, but without breaking and entering; forgery) Serious violations of rules: 13) often stays out at night despite parental prohibitions, beginning before age 13 years 14) has run away from home overnight at least twice while living in parental or parental surrogate home (or once without returning for a lengthy period) 15) often truant from school, beginning before age 13 years (APA, 2000, 66–7).

Children who are suspecting of having CD and who perpetrate bullying, and additionally present with limited empathy for their targets, or guilt related to bullying behavior may need more intensive intervention. Most research needs to be conducted on children displaying these characteristics with particular attention on what interventions are effective. Of particular concern are children who admit enjoyment and satisfaction from bullying and making their peers cry. The fifth edition of the Diagnostic and Statistical Manual of Mental Disorders (DSM-5) added a specifier during the revision process to the DSM-4 adding to the descriptor to those having full diagnosis of the disorder. The specifier applies to those individuals with a more serious pattern of behavior characterized by a callous and unemotional interpersonal style across multiple settings and relationships. The specifier goes beyond the presence of negative behavior and reflects an individual's typical patterns in emotional and interpersonal functioning. People with CD who show this specifier display limited empathy and little concern for the feelings, wishes, and well-being of others.

CONDUCT DISORDER AND CALLOUS-UNEMOTIONAL (CU) TRAITS

White et al. (2013) suggest the presence of CU traits designates an important subgroup of youth demonstrating more severe and chronic antisocial behavior. Bullying has been linked to higher levels of CU traits that in males and females include lack of guilt, lack of empathy, poor affect and use of another for personal gain (Barry et al. 2000; Viding et al. 2009). Pardini et al. (2012) studying young girls to examine the utility of the CU subtype of CD in the DSM-5, hypothesized that those having the CU subtype of CD would have more severe antisocial behaviors than those with CD alone. They found that girls with the CU subtype of CD demonstrated higher levels of externalizing symptoms, bullying, relational aggression, and global impairment than girls with CD alone.

Bullying behaviors also can be resistant to change, with some children not responding to treatment. Masi et al. (2014) studying boys (mean age 11 years old) found nearly half referred for treatment did not respond to multimodal treatment. Those presenting with callous-unemotional (CU) traits at baseline were predicted to be non-responders. This study suggests the importance of identifying CU traits and associated psychopathology early on in order to identify children likely to be unresponsive to treatment.

OTHER CORRELATES

In a nationally representative survey of U.S. children in the 6th through 10th grades, Shetgiri et al. (2012) found children at greatest risk for bullying had above-average academic performance, moderate-to-high family affluence, daily feelings of irritability, are frequently involved in other antisocial, violent behavior such as weapon-carrying (Cunningham, et al. 2000), school dropout, poor achievement (Byrne 1994; Haynie et al. 2001; Nansel et al. 2001; Olweus 1993), drank alcohol, and smoked (Nansel 2001). Houghton, Nathan, and Taylor (2012) found similar results when they studied twenty-eight adolescent students suspended from school for bullying. Results indicated students who bullied expressed they deliberately chose to bully to attain a reputation and used cyberbullying to deliberately instill a sense of fear in their victims. Most attended 6th and 8th grades, were male, tobacco smokers, and were teased by families about their appearance.

Velki (2012) studied individual characteristics and the contexts in which Croatian children were involved in bullying, finding that both males and females were involved equally as bullies and victims. Children who bullied were found to have less empathy, higher impulsivity, were found to use the Internet, play computer games, and watch television more. Both children who bullied and victims had parents who used negative discipline and lacked close relationships with them. Children who bullied perceived that making friends was easy and had friends who were not bullies. Noninvolved children were most accepted by peers compared to children who bullied and children who were victims. Victims were least accepted, isolated and without a social network to rely on, becoming easy targets. While children who bullied did not have poorer school performance compared to noninvolved children, victims had poorer academic achievement.

PARENTAL AND FAMILY PREDICTORS

Research consistently demonstrates children who bully are from families where there is lack of warmth and involvement, lack of appropriate supervision, and inconsistent physical discipline (Duncan 2004; Olweus 1993; Olweus et al. 1999; Rigby 1993, 1994). Cooper and Nickerson (2013) examined parental recollections of bullying involvement and their current views and abilities to cope with bullying in their own children finding although few parents were involved as bully perpetrators, 90.3% reported seeing and/or engaging in bullying.

Shetgiri et al. (2002) examining associations among child, parent, and community factors and bullying perpetration among children aged 10 to 17 years found that African American and Latino children and children living in poverty with emotional, developmental, or behavioral (EDB) problems had higher odds of bullying. Parents who were angry and felt their child bothered them a lot or was hard to care for also had children who bullied more. Children who bully are found to have more exposure to domestic violence (Baldry

2003) and are maltreated (Shields and Cicchetti 2001). Studying the effects of childhood exposure to physical punishment and later victimization in school, Björkqvist and Österman (2014) found a relationship to future victimization, and perpetration of aggression. Parents who talked with their children and met their friends had reduced odds of their children being bullied, again indicating the benefits of schools supporting the child and the relationship with their parents (Shetgiri, Lin, and Flores 2013).

One teacher shares her insights:

> How a child is raised in the home can provide a lot of insight as to why he or she behaves a certain way. When meeting with parents, I have usually found that nice, caring moms and dads raise nice, caring children. Children with unconcerned or problematic parents tend to reflect their attitudes or behaviors. We have to remember that it is not the child's fault and he or she deserves the support from an educational team to do what is best. If that child is a bully, getting to the root of the problem is our job. I have been fortunate enough have not witnessed chronic bullying directly in my few years as a teacher however I do understand there is usually never enough time to deal with this.

Children who bully are from families having a history of antisocial behavior (Vaughn et al. 2010) where parents are authoritarian, hostile, inconsistent in discipline (Henry 2004) and parenting practices are dysfunctional (Reid et al. 2002). Lereya, Samara and Wolfe (2013) studying the relationship of parenting behavior and the risk of become a victim and a bully/victim, found negative parenting behavior to be related to increased risk for becoming a bully/victim. Mustanoja et al. (2011) exploring the relationship of domestic violence and violence occurring outside the home to bullying behavior in a sample of psychiatric inpatient adolescents found that males witnessing inter-parental violence were at an increased risk of being victims, while females who were victims of violent crimes had an increased risk of becoming bully-victims.

Abused children may become bully-victims, becoming submissive and ingratiating with their parents in order to maintain their safety in violent homes (Finkelhor and Browne, 1985; Koenig, Cicchetti, and Rogosch 2000). Li, Putalaz, and Su (2011) studying interparental conflict styles found a relationship to their Chinese children's aggression, finding boys coming from families where fathers are coercive and controlling to be more aggressive. Melander, Hartshorn, and Whitback (2013) exploring the relationship between familial, educational and psychosocial factors and bullying among 702 North American indigenous adolescents, found students who bullied were angrier, had poorer relationships with parents, and poorer academic achievement compared to victims, and learned aggressive interactions at home.

A teacher shares his views on parenting and bullying others:

> One example that comes to mind is a fourth grade student whispering racial slurs to another student. This student was quoted telling a Hispanic student to "go back to his country." The situation was handled based on my school's Code of Conduct, but much was not done outside of disciplining the immediate incident. When asked for a reason as to why he acted in this way, the student said, "my parents don't like Spanish people." Although the parents did not condone what their child said, it is likely that little discipline was used at home.

Hemphill et al. (2012) conducting a longitudinal analysis of predictors of cyber and traditional bullying perpetration among Australian adolescents, found family conflict predictive of traditional forms of bullying while students with more parental support were less involved in bullying (Wang, Iannotti, and Nansel 2009). Hong et al. (2012) studying the association of childhood maltreatment to school bullying found emotional dysregulation, depression, anger, and social skill deficits as potential mediators and quality of parent-child relationships, peer relationships, and teacher relationships as potential moderators. Results suggest interventions improving these factors may have effects on reducing child maltreatment. Espelage et al. (2013) studying relationships between family violence, fighting, bullying, and substance use, found as "boys are exposed to greater levels of family conflict, they engage in increasing levels of aggression directed toward their peers" and "greater levels of substance use," whereas "girls exposed to high levels of family violence report greater alcohol and drug use over time" (10). Also, parental absence may account for emotional deprivation, causing a marked increase in aggression among young children (McAdams and Lambie 2003) also suggesting the importance of enhancing the development of healthy relationships between parents and their children.

GENDER PREDICTOR

Frequently, males are portrayed as bully perpetrators and aggressors (Juvonen et al. 2003) while females are portrayed as indirect and relational aggressors. Gender stereotypical traits and gender perspective among secondary school students were studied in Spain (Navarro, Larranaga, and Yubero 2010). Both males and females having higher scores for masculine gender traits engaged more in psychological, verbal and social exclusion bullying while those with higher feminine traits engaged less in bullying. This study implies that gender perspective also needs to be utilized in anti-bullying initiatives with the realization that both males and females engage in overt and covert types of bullying. Interestingly, higher feminine traits were negatively correlated with bully perpetration and linked to males' victimization. Fans and Fehnlee (2011) indicated males are motivated to demonstrate masculinity, and both males and females are motivated to establish a place within their gender hierarchies.

Research identifies bullying as largely a male phenomenon (Wang, Iannotti, and Nansel 2009). Hamby, Finkelhor, and Turner (2013) studied gender patterns for 21 forms of youth victimization performing a U.S. study in children aged one month to 17 years of age in the U.S. Male perpetration was more common for physical assault whereas higher percentages of female-on-female incidences were associated with verbal victimization. The stereotype of exclusive female perpetration of verbal and relational aggression was challenged, however finding smaller gender differences than previously thought for verbal aggression and social exclusion.

CONCEPTUALIZATION OF THE BULLY-VICTIM DYAD

Although bullying is currently thought of as a group process, some evidence finds that victimization by male or female perpetrators is not random. Perpetrators develop bully-victim dyads and aggressor-victim relationships (Card 2011), and children bully peers because they desire both domination and social approval (Veenstra et al. 2007). They were most likely to be boys, who were dominantly aggressive and accepted by peers because they typically did not pick targets when risking getting rejected for doing so. "Targets are rejected children whom one can bully with impunity" (18). This study suggests teachers provide alternate status opportunities for those who bully while encouraging friends to stand up for the victim. Attaching positive status to standing up and negative status for bullying may be effective in bully reduction.

BULLY PERPETRATORS WHO ARE FEMALE

Covert bullying among females has been recognized as a social behavioral problem for many generations.

A teacher reports:

Looking back on elementary school days, it is baffling that one girl had an uncanny and amazing ability to exert a tremendous power over peers who desperately wanted her approval. Covertly and successfully, she managed to exclude many and include selected others in her close-knit circle. Although she was *relentless* in efforts to exert her power, and would make quiet and disparaging remarks about peers and teachers, she did well academically, was athletic, and liked by many teachers who were unaware of her bullying behaviors. Parents in the community however were very aware because their children reported her hurtful behaviors. Looking back on those early days and having the perspective now, it is clear that her manipulation and subtle tactics enabled her to exert tremendous power over others in order to feel good and get what she desired.

Another female teacher shares her experience in school and later as an adult:

I have been affected by bullying once in my life. It happened to me in the ninth grade. Years ago we had junior high and it was from 7th to 9th grade. Unfortunately, our new school was not ready when I entered 9th grade. My experience with bullying started the first day at lunch. None of my close friends were in my lunch period. I had to search for a table full of girls that I could sit with. I was happy when I saw Sandra and walked over to her with my tray in hand and started to talk to her. I found myself getting the message rather quickly from a girl named Meaghan that I was not wanted. Now had I sat down Sandra would have welcomed me, but Meaghan's silent nasty mean presence and snotty look was so much more clear than Sandra's acceptance. I took my lunch and sat by myself. I found a girl that transferred from a Catholic school who felt misplaced and we sat together for the rest of that year. I was a friendly girl with lots of friends, but not at lunch. I dreaded lunch that year, and have to admit that it still hurts. It seems that it is difficult to get over such rejection. There is a happy ending to my story. Meaghan, the mean girl sought me out at my 20th high school reunion. She was not with any of her friends, felt uncomfortable and sat at a table with my friends and me. The 14 year old in me wanted to embarrass her in front of her husband, but the adult in me realized that this girl who was now 38 years old had no real power over me. I didn't want to act the same way she did to me so many years ago. I have told my children this story more than once and instilled in them to always be kind no matter what. I wanted them to know that our less honorable actions can affect us for a lifetime.

Bully perpetration in females and relational aggression began with the notion of "Really Mean Girls (RMG)," "Queen Bees," or "Alpha Girls," (Wiseman, as cited in Talbot 2002) the "ones who are supposed to own up to having back-stabbed or dumped a friend, but they are also the most resistant to the exercise and the most self-justifying." Current views are not significantly different. Female-on-female aggression is primarily through verbal victimization (Hamby, Finkelhor, and Turner 2013) and nonverbal social aggression (Blake, Kim, and Lease 2011) with females more likely to be involved in relational bullying (Wang, Iannotti and Nansel, 2009).

One research study examines the relationship between maternal control, children's concerns for others and female aggression. McGrath and Zook (2010) found high maternal control to be associated with lower empathy in girls suggesting that girls appear to need less direct, instructive style than boys. Girls already having internalized feelings and behaviors that reflect concern for others, and mothers who have high control may be undermining their daughters' intrinsic motivation to show empathy (62).

Conceptualization of friendships in females is different than in males, implying that bullying interventions need to be tailored by gender. Besag (2006) studying patterns of instability in friendship bonds in girls between ten and 12 years old, found they consider their friendships to be of *extreme* importance, with the breaking of a friendship as the most anxiety-provoking aspect of school life.

CONTEXTUAL FACTORS: ETHNICITY, SOCIOECONOMIC STATUS (SES), URBANICITY, AND SCHOOL ENVIRONMENT

Contextual factors such as ethnicity, socioeconomic status, urbanicity, and school environment have been examined for relationships to bullying. Bradshaw et al. (2013) studied 16,302 adolescents (50.3% female, 62.2% Caucasian, 37.8% African American) enrolled in 52 high schools finding urban and African American high school youth who were bullies and bully-victims to be at greatest of risk of being involved in violence, engaging in multiple types of substance use, and having academic problems. Goldweber, Waasdorp and Bradshaw (2013) found bully-victims in urban schools were most likely to bully for money. Pousels and Cillessen (2013) examining correlates and outcomes associated with aggression and victimization among 1st, 2nd, and 3rd grade elementary school children and low-income urban contexts found early aggression and victimization to be associated with initial behavioral and relational problems, with early aggression predicting later behavioral and relational problems in adolescence. Findings indicate the importance of taking a developmental perspective of aggression among young elementary school children in contexts of low-income urban environments.

Tippett, Wolke, and Platt (2013) studied ethnic differences in bullying involvement among a UK sample of adolescents finding little difference in perpetration or victimization across ethnic groups while Tippett and Wolke (2014) looked at the association between roles in bullying and socioeconomic status finding only a weak relationship. Victims and bully-victims were more likely to come from households with low socioeconomic status with bullies and victims slightly less likely to come from high socioeconomic backgrounds. This study indicates interventions should be targeted toward all schools and students regardless of SES.

Research has examined the correlation between bullying behavior and variables in school environments. In school, children who bully tend to associate with other aggressive children and where school staff is indifferent (Olweus 1993), where there is lax adult supervision (Boulton and Smith 1994; Pellegrini and Bartini 2000; Olweus 1993, Smith and Sharp 1994) and where teachers are ineffective in maintaining control. Elsaesser, Gorman-Smith, and Henry (2013) examining the risk for involvement in relational aggression and victimization among 5,625 urban minority middle school youth (49.2% female) found no school-level indicator of climate to be related to relational aggression or victimization. In this study, a student's individual beliefs about aggression and individual perceptions of the school environment were related strongly to both the perpetration of and victimization by relational aggression.

AGGRESSION AND RISK FACTORS IN CHILDREN (BIRTH THROUGH AGE EIGHT)

The most important time to consider prevention of aggression and bullying behavior is during the preschool and early childhood years. "Bullies are well embedded in their kindergarten group and therefore do not have fewer friends than noninvolved children. They tend to affiliate with other bullies" (Vlachou et al. 2011, 344). "Preschool may be the first context beyond the home environment where children's difficulties in social interactions with peers can be primarily detected and assessed by adults and professionals" (329). Unfortunately, preschool teachers have minimal knowledge and training in behavior management, parents deny the problem, pediatricians ignore or diagnose the child incorrectly, and there is lack of collaboration between preschool programs, parents, and medical providers.

There are also deficiencies in the research on studies of bullying during preschool. Evidence exists that acting aggressively and being the target are common occurrences among young preschool and kindergarten children (Hanish et al. 2004, 144) where children are likely to be both aggressive bullies and victims. As they age, these two groups tend to become more distinct. Interventions and responses need to focus on reducing all aggressive acts among young children. Preschool teachers, often underpaid and unrecognized, are essential in the early intervention process.

Identifying early risk factors predictive of problematic behavior disorders in young children, and applying principles of behavior and working with the family, may significantly affect prognosis of children at risk for bullying. A study examining previously established risk factors for problem behavior among kindergarten and 1st-grade children at risk for EBD determined which of these factors would best predict problem behavior (Nelson et al. 2007). Five risk factors best predicted borderline/clinical levels of problem behavior including destroying own toys, difficulty sleeping, physically abusive to others, being a difficult child, and maternal depression. A child who destroys their own toys has been associated with aggression, peer problems and having trouble in school in previous studies (Walker et al. 1990) with maternal depression also a well-documented variable associated with behavior problems in young children (Papp 2004). Intervention planning should include parent training and supports for parents having difficult children and recommendations from providers for mothers having depression.

Many parents are not aware that resources may be available to assist with a very difficult child. Children should be referred to Early Intervention (birth through 2 years) or a multidisciplinary team for evaluation under IDEA (age 3–21) for possible behavioral and psychological services under an Individualized Family Service Plan (IFSP) or IEP if behaviors persist. The urgency for early behavioral intervention is critical because research suggests interventions implemented after age eight may have little effect on bullying behaviors in children (Olweus 1993).

Nelson et al. (2013) studied possible associations between parents' psychological control and Russian preschoolers' physical and relational aggression. Children's aggression (mostly in opposite gender dyads) was positively related to parental dimensions of control including shaming, constraining verbal expressions, invalidating feelings, love withdrawal, and guilt induction. Emond et al. (2007) studying preschool behaviors and social-cognitive problems as predictors of disruptive behaviors, and then ODD and aggressive conduct disorder (ACD) during adolescence, found difficult behaviors in preschool children included having a temper, being disobedient, bossy, and being a child who bullied. Only bullying significantly predicted adolescent ACD and all other behaviors predicted ODD.

Other evidence suggests links between aggression and early-onset CD in young children with associated factors including hostile parenting, frequency and severity of conduct symptoms, ADHD symptoms, and poor reading ability (Scott et al. 2010, 49). Externalizing and aggressive behaviors present should be given serious attention because, "At least 50% of preschool-age children with moderate-to-severe externalizing problems continued to show some degree of disturbance at school age, with boys' problems more severe than girls' behavior" (Webster-Stratton 1996, 540).

Although aggression and bullying behaviors are sometimes recognized as two different constructs, teachers during preschool and the early years need to be diligent in addressing possible risk factors, given the association between childhood aggression and bullying later in school. Considering characteristics, correlates, and risk factors of children who perpetrate bullying serves not to stigmatize or blame, but to provide early and necessary interventions. For a small percentage of students, this may be their only chance of positive outcomes later in life.

Chapter 4

Cyberbullying and Relationship between Bullying and Mental Health

The process of bullying now runs faceless (Maag 2007) and has evolved due to rapid advances in technology, and numerous electronic devices available to youth. Smartphones, Facebook, Twitter, Instagram, YouTube, and apps such as Yik Yak, allow for immediate and anonymous bullying. Anonymity, coupled with a lack of educational and parental cyber monitoring, and use of global positioning devices (GPS) provides youth with the potential to track a peer's every move and text anything desired to any other individual or group.

DEFINITION OF CYBERBULLYING

Cyberbullying, also known as electronic bullying, is an intentional, aggressive behavior performed through electronic means (Hinduja and Patchin 2009). Cyberbullying is differentiated from cybercrime, also an international problem involving hacking into computers and electronic information and using malware or computer viruses to destroy computer files (Marcum et al. 2014). Lives worldwide are becoming increasingly transparent where no one enjoys the privacy they perceive due to hidden surveillance systems, drones, and electronics.

Research suggests victims of both cyberbullying and traditional school bullying have the highest risk for suicide (Messias, Kindrick, and Castro 2014). Involvement in cyberbullying as either a victim or a bully is associated with both depression and suicidal ideation "over and above the contribution of involvement in traditional forms of bullying," suggesting cyberbullying to be a unique phenomenon needing further study (Bonanno and Hymel 2013).

Unfortunately, cyberbullying may get worse before it gets better due to rapid advances in technology and the inability of school districts, law enforcement and judicial systems to match its pace, putting all students at risk. No matter how technologically savvy individuals are, many are vulnerable to cyber-victimization, but most at risk are youth who desperately want validation from their peers, and do not possess the self-restraint to stay unharmed. Fryling et al. (2015) examined cyberbullying in online gaming environments finding males to be more likely to exhibit bullying behavior. Male and female victims who experienced repeated cyberbullying instances had an increase in aggressive and cyberbullying behavior with females more likely to be affected psychologically.

Students are very concerned by cyberbullying, as demonstrated by a Nigerian study (Oyewusi and Orolade 2014). They found students while not bothered by cyberbullying in the classroom were disturbed by its effects outside of school. Society's emotional response is illustrated by reactions to the YouTube clip of a boy with autism, thinking he was participating in the amyotrophic lateral sclerosis (ALS) challenge and having a bucket of excrement (instead of ice water) poured over his head by youth thinking the act was funny. Parents, often unaware of their child's behavior and not considering the potential detrimental effects of technology, unknowingly may provide them with social arsenals to inflict harm on peers.

As described by one female:

> One app, called Yik Yak, serves as such a medium for bullying and I initially heard of it from a 16-year-old coworker at my summer job. After she briefly explained the popular app and the damage it has caused to her close friends I was horrified that such a program would exist. Not only does the application provide its users with complete anonymity, but it serves as a twitter 'venting feed' on which users can connect with other anonymous persons in his/her area (using GPS location data). This feature enabled the app to be used as a cruel bulletin board filled with the local gossip of the small high school I once attended. In the particular case of my coworker, she was upset because there were numerous postings over a significant length of time saying horrible things about her close friend. Later on, she found out that these postings were actually typed by another of one of their close friends, putting her in an extremely uncomfortable situation. This example of cyber bullying showed me how much drama and harassment between high-school-aged girls has morphed into a new form of 'masked' bullying since I was in school.

Of the electronic devices available, Hindija and Patchin (2015) found cell phones and other mobile devices to be the most popular technology with large numbers of middle school students using Instagram and Facebook. Spreading rumors was found to be the most common form of cyberbullying with approximately 34% of middle school students experiencing cyberbullying and 15% cyberbullying others in their lifetimes. Females are more likely to experience cyberbullying (40.6% vs. 28.2%) and both boys (15.5%) and girls (14.0%) are equally likely to report it. Contrary to popular opinion, not every teen is engaging in cyberbullying, but nevertheless, evidence suggests it is on the increase with 30% of teens having been targets, up from 24% 10 years prior (Hinduja and Patchin 2014). Similarly, 19% reported having cyberbullied others, demonstrating an increase from 17% in earlier studies. Teens who bully others in person are more than twice as likely to bully others online and kids who had been bullied in person were almost three times as likely to be cyberbullied (Hinduja and Patchin, 2014, 18). Studying 177 grade-seven students, Li (2007) found almost 54% were victims of traditional bullying and over a quarter of them had been cyberbullied. Almost one in three students had bullied others in the traditional form, and almost 15% had bullied others using electronic communication tools. Almost 60% of the cyber victims were female while over 52% of cyberbullies were male with the majority of victims and bystanders not reporting incidents to adults.

Mitchell et al. (2015) studying peer harassment incidents among youth found 54% of bullying took place in person, 15% through technology, and 31% occurred both in person and through technology. The most common types of online harassment included text messaging, followed by social networking, with 88% of all harassment incidents involving a physical or social power imbalance when the incident began. Technology-only harassment incidents were found to be significantly less distressing to victims than in-person harassment incidents. Youth reported that technology-only incidents were easier to stop than those that occurred solely in person (8–9).

DIFFERENCES FROM FACE-TO-FACE BULLYING

Cyberbullying may be an entirely different phenomenon compared to traditional forms of bullying, given the aspect of disinhibition, where individuals self-disclose or act out more frequently or intensely than they would in person (Suler 2004). Students who may not otherwise bully a peer face-to-face, will engage in online bullying because they think it is acceptable, feel invisible, can hide behind their online personalities, and believe it unlikely they will be caught. They generally do not see the pain of their victim(s), absolving them of the responsibility to demonstrate empathy. Additionally, it seems that everyone is doing it, implying that social norms promote online misbehavior. More introverted students may feel more comfortable communicating online especially when feeling justified in retaliating against a peer (Willard, n.d). Disinhibition, coupled with the nature of adolescence, sophistication of technology, and naiveté of parents and teachers, make for a dangerous combination.

RELATIONSHIP BETWEEN TRADITIONAL
AND CYBERBULLYING

Cuervo et al. (2014) found a relationship between traditional and cyber aggression among Mexican high school students with frequencies ranging from 3% to 16.2%. Studying types of technology used including sending offensive messages, threatening, spreading rumors, invading privacy through spreading secrets or private images, social exclusion from network groups such as blocking, and impersonating the identity of the victim, students reported denigrating or spreading rumors and harassing though sending offensive messages to their victims as most common means of cyberbullying peers. Research demonstrates cyber aggressors have skills in understanding the mental states of others, and use this ability to victimize them (Sutton, Smith, and Swettenham 1999) and elevate their social power (Sijtsema et al. 2009).

Research has also examined how cyberbullying differs from traditional bullying (relational, verbal, and physical). Waasdorp and Bradshaw (2015) found 23% of youth reported being victims of any form of bullying, with 25.6% of those victims reporting being cyberbullied. Of the victims, 4.6% reported being only cyberbullied and typically believed the perpetrator to be a friend. This study implies that electronic bullying is most likely to occur with other forms of bullying and similar to traditional victims, cyberbullied youth were at increased risk for experiencing multiple forms of bullying, especially relational forms, and for reporting higher level of internalizing and externalizing symptoms.

PREDICTORS OF CYBERBULLYING

The research base on predictors of cyberbullying is still developing. Modecki, Barber, and Vernon (2013) studied predictors of cyber-perpetration and the trajectory of bullying and victimization among youth in grades 8 through 10 and later in grade 11. Examining the relationship between problem behavior, self-esteem and depressed mood and its association to cyber-perpetration and victimization, an increase in problem behaviors during the early grades predicted both cyber-perpetration and victimization later. Decreases in self-esteem predicted both grade 11 perpetration and victimization, and depressed mood predicted both perpetration and victimization later on. The relationship found indicates a need to respond to early behavioral risk in order to prevent cyberbullying later in high school.

A two-year Korean longitudinal study (Yang et al. 2013) found cyberbullying to have different predictors compared to traditional bullying. Male gender and depressive symptoms were associated with all types of bullying, while living with a single parent was associated with perpetration of traditional bullying. Bullying with higher ADHD symptoms was associated with victimization while students with lower academic achievement, anxiety, and self-esteem were associated with cyberbullying perpetration and victimization. Data suggest students who may be traditional victims of bullying having low self-esteem, anxiety, and depression may be the ones engaging in cyberbully perpetration.

GENDER ISSUES

Cyberbullying involves a form of indirect harassment. The assumption is that females, being more verbal and more indirect compared to males may predispose their involvement in cyberbullying. Marcum et al. (2014) explored gender relationships and predictors of using Facebook to hurt others studying the variables of parent attachment, school commitment, and low self-control. Also studied were number of hours using social networking sites and email, number of friends using the devices, age, sex, renting or dormitory living, and being victimized by another with the intent to hurt. Females (9%) and males (9%) were *equally* likely to cyberbully using Facebook to post hurtful comments. Furthermore, males and females with lower levels of self-control and those who were victims were more likely to cyberbully. In males, more hours on social networking sites predicted more cyberbullying and with females, more friends using social networking predicted participation in spreading online gossip via Facebook.

CONCEPTUALIZATION OF "DRAMA"

A qualitative study (Allen 2014) conducted on a mother and her 15-year-old daughter, a popular cheerleader attending a suburban high school, explored the conceptualization of adolescent social drama. As the interview unfolds, the researcher expresses feeling appalled, disempowered, manipulated, and deceived by the daughter's apparent warmth and friendliness while learning about her actions during the "drama." Studying the phenomenon, she discovers "drama" as sharing too much information with others (i.e., tweeting, texting, Facebook), the involvement in someone else's private business allowing for its permanent existence, and individual's ability to stir the pot and restart the old drama.

Findings from this study shed light on the complicated processes of the group dynamic while jockeying for positions at the top of the peer group.

Drama is an "emergent construct, conceptualized as social interactions characterized by overreaction, exaggeration, excessive emotionality, prolongation, inclusion of extraneous individuals, inflated importance, and temporary relevance" (Allen 2014). Cyberbullying often includes all of these variables interfering with the educational process.

INFLUENCE OF SOCIAL STANDING

Bullying research consistently demonstrates victims are vulnerable individuals with less power compared to those who bully. This may not be the case with cyberbullying, where everyone is a potential victim. Examining the associations between electronic aggression and victimization with social standing among 9th grade youth at two different time periods, Badaly et al. (2013) found more popular youth to be electronically aggressive and victimized, with popularity associated with increases in electronic aggression over time. These findings suggest popular youth are at increased risk for electronic victimization as students utilize technology to establish themselves in the social hierarchy and maintain this status among peers.

ATTITUDES OF STUDENTS ABOUT VICTIMS
AND TEACHERS' ABILITY TO INTERVENE

Elledge et al. (2013) examined whether children's attitudes (pro-victim) and perceptions of their teachers' classroom behavior influenced cyberbullying. Studying Finnish students in grades 3 to 5 and again in grades 7 and 8, students who had positive attitudes about victims of bullying were less likely to cyberbully and their perceptions of the teachers' ability to intervene was associated with higher levels of indirect and covert forms of bullying. These findings suggest parental and community support is needed to monitor children's online activities because teachers who are effective in discouraging bullying in the classroom have the effect of increasing cyberbullying. This troubling finding also suggests that bullying prevention needs to include strong measures to decrease cyberbullying, and that responsibility largely falls to parents.

RISK AND PROTECTIVE FACTORS OF PARENTS

A longitudinal study examining individual, peer, family and school risk factors for both cyber and traditional bullying among Australian adolescent youth (Hemphill, et al. 2012) found 15% of students engaged in cyberbullying, 21% in traditional bullying, and 7% engaged in both. While traditional bullying was more prevalent in boys compared to girls, no gender differences were found for cyberbullying. Traditional bullying, relational aggression, interaction with antisocial friends, poor family management, family conflict, academic failure, and low commitment to school were all associated with increases in cyberbullying later on. This study indicates anti-bullying efforts need to include efforts to address family conflict, provide student academic support and monitor friendships.

Protective factors of cyberbullying have also been studied. Adolescents who feared consequences from parents engaged less in cyberbullying while those who had peers engaging in cyberbullying were more likely to participate (Hinduja and Patchin, 2013). Accordino and Accordino (2011) found students with strong and close, rather than distant relationships with their parents were cyberbullied less frequently.

What can parents and teachers suggest youth do if they are being cyberbullied? Hinduja and Patchin (2014) suggest ten ways to deal with and respond to cyberbullying, (1) Keep a journal, responding to who, what, where and how did it make you feel? (2) Save the evidence by taking and saving screenshots (3) Never retaliate (4) Talk about it (5) Ignore it (6) Laugh it off (7) Speak up and tell the person to stop (8) Block the bullying (9) Report it to social media sites (10) Tell an adult and call the police when your safety (or the safety of someone else) is in jeopardy (30–36).

Online bullying is less distressing and less common compared to in-person bullying (Mitchell et al. 2015) but still has significant consequences for perpetrators, victims, educators, and families. Males and females with lower levels of self-control are more likely to cyberbully by posting hurtful messages or pictures to Facebook without stopping to consider the repercussions. Females who have an increased number of friends using social networking websites increased the likelihood of participating in cyberbullying via Facebook gossip (Marcum et al. 2014). Parents and educators share responsibility for keeping children safe but this can be a challenge because both children who cyberbully and their victims are reluctant to tell parents, fearing their devices will be taken away. Realistically, students will find ways to utilize technology, therefore parents need to aggressively become as educated as their children in all aspects of technology and social media, employing and enabling blocking features and parental controls. Parents readily pay for cell phone family share plans and Internet fees for devices, but forget that their children's cell phone and computer use are privileges. Parents forget their child can both earn and have Smartphone and computer time taken away. Enticing and exciting as devices are, parents and schools might seriously consider curtailing use of smart phones and other devices especially when a child is found to demonstrate bullying behavior or is consistently victimized. Bullying and ill effects of unmonitored social media can be substantially disruptive to the education process and a distraction from student learning. Educators and parents need to thoroughly investigate bullying incidences and keep all evidence. Occasionally, it may be appropriate to contact attorneys, cell phone providers, or web environments such as Facebook to remove offensive content or threats because cyberbullying may be beyond the purview of schools (Hinduja and Patchin 2015). Educators, parents, school boards, and attorneys need to continually reevaluate their school district codes of conduct related to the appropriate use of smartphones and other devices in school.

Cyberbullying has received much attention by schools and the media and perceived as very damaging to youth. It is important to stay focused on the most pressing problems; examination of the research indicates *in-person* and mixed harassment may be more problematic than cyberbullying. Prevention programs that teach youth to handle negative feelings and to de-escalate tensions are promising as the sophistication of social emotional learning programs develop (Mitchell 2015).

RELATIONSHIP BETWEEN BULLYING AND MENTAL HEALTH

Mental health of youth and young adults is beginning to receive national attention, however the majority of research on bullying and mental health has been conducted in Europe and Australia. In the United States, the Substance Abuse and Mental Health Services Administration (SAMHSA) offers State Education Agencies Project Aware Grants designed to build and expand the capacity to increase awareness of mental health issues in children and connect youth and families to appropriate services (www.samhsa.gov). Mental health issues are pervasive with nearly half of young adults (18–25) not receiving mental health services (Merikangas et al. 2011) although they felt they needed them. Explanation for not receiving services included, cost, fear of discrimination from employers, family or friends, feeling they had a low perceived need, or the notion that treatment would not help.

The discussion of bullying needs to coincide with discussions of mental health because the diagnosis of a mental health disorder such as depression, anxiety, and ADHD is strongly associated with being identified as a bully (Benedict, et al. 2014). In 2007, 15.2% of U.S. children between the age of 6 an 17 years were identified as bullies and 14.9% carried a diagnosis of at least one mental health disorder (Benedict, 2014, 5) with the majority (64.4%) being males. Fifteen percent of children in the United States were identified as bullies by their parents. Bullies should be given mental health resources and children with mental health disorders should be screened for bullying behavior. This may serve to ensure the health and safety of those who bully, victims and bully-victims (10).

Victims of bullying are also at risk for psychotic experiences in early adolescence. Wolke et al. (2014) studying children between ages eight and eleven years and then again at 18 years found "involvement in bullying, whether as victim, bully/victim or bully may increase the risk of developing psychotic experiences in adolescence" (2199). They also found bully-victims had the greatest risk for psychotic experiences compared to victims, with significant association between being a pure bully and psychotic experiences. Additionally, children who were chronically bullied were more likely to have psychotic experiences compared to those only bullied at one point in time. Furthermore, some children who are bullied or bully in elementary school may not develop other mental health problems such as depression prior to showing psychotic experiences. Children were also found to report being victimized more often than their parents reported, suggesting that victims often suffer in silence (2205). The findings suggest health professionals routinely ask children and parents about bullying of and by peers. Guidance counselors and psychologists cannot possibly deliver the type or intensity, or duration of services needed for nearly one-fifth of the school population.

One-fifth of the U.S. population attends or works in schools. Providing appropriate mental health services for children who need them has the potential for improving outcomes for many students. As it stands now, the school system can be considered the de facto mental health system for children in this country. Federal policies to implement school-based mental health (SBMH) services have been around for some time. These initiatives may significantly increase the number of children in need who receive services, and subsequently improve a range of outcomes including social and emotional functioning, and academic progress. However, in the case of SBMH, federal and state agencies can address the issue of low levels of implementation by providing leadership for local communities. Good policies require a delineation of specific procedures and support in order for those implementing them to provide and sustain their programs.

Planning for every aspect of a child's life is an impossible task for parents, but many at least, customarily prepare for such events as giving birth, selecting a pediatrician, registering their child for school, and signing up their child for activities. Books are plentiful on feeding, toilet training, and child development and parents often share ideas with ease. Most however are ill-prepared to deal and discuss mental health needs that often appear at some time in their child's lives. While inclined to share physical concerns with friends, relatives and pediatricians, discussion about their child's struggles with depression, anxiety, or severe behaviors is taboo. Educators also are not prepared especially in cases where the student is quiet, passive and mental health problems go unnoticed. Society's reticence to seriously discuss child mental health, lack of education and awareness of the problem, and lack of honestly accompanying societal stigma put children in emotional jeopardy.

Bullying in early childhood has also been studied from a social justice perspective, where it is recognized that the child has rights to develop to their capacity, and schools have the responsibility to protect the child from harm. Halpern et al. (2015) performed an analysis of research studies showing that early subordination in children by the age of five and the formation of social hierarchies has a harmful effect. "Within weeks of beginning preschool, children form stable social hierarchies, where subsets of children perceived as shy, passive, sensitive, or awkward, are routinely subordinated" (528). "Sensitive children subjected to unfettered dominance by peers develop more extreme and enduring patterns of stress reactivity, putting them at risk for future bullying and exclusion" (Halpern, 526). Kim et al (2015) demonstrated early marginalization makes children vulnerable to ongoing peer victimization and bullying, resulting in long-term mental and physical harm with some exhibiting preexisting physiologic sensitivity to stress (Strayer and Trudel 1984). From a social justice perspective, it is recognized that children have fundamental rights to protection from social harm and the right to a good future where their capacity is not diminished. Social institutions such as schools are recognized as having a fiduciary responsibility to keep children protected from harm including both bodily and *social* harm (Halpern et al. 2015). Educators have the responsibility of preventing "damaging dominance hierarchies, enabling children to develop a healthy sense of self-efficacy and normal physiologic capabilities . . ." (Halpern, 2015, 528).

Two federal laws include language on emotional health. IDEA focuses on students who have an identifiable disability that affects their educational achievement. Children who have an emotional disability usually receive school-based counseling once or twice a week, have behavior intervention plans, are placed in appropriate settings to meeting their needs. Unfortunately, many children who have emotional disturbance are not identified and therefore do not receive services. Findings from the Special Education Elementary Longitudinal Study (SEELS) and the National Longitudinal and Transition study 2 (NLTS2) found outcomes of children who have emotional disturbances are the poorest of all disability groups, with less than half receiving mental health services in schools and few in community mental health agencies.

No Child Left Behind (NCLB, 2002) also addresses the emotional well-being of all children. Given that 20% of all children will have a diagnosable mental illness at a level of impairment at some point (Kutash et al., 2005) schools are challenged to provide the mental health supports needed. Although interagency collaboration is encouraged to enhance service capacity, federal policy gives little direction on how to collaborate and deliver effective SBMH services. Federal and state governments, schools, and mental health agencies essentially do not speak the same language and do not know how to work together.

Legal anti-bullying requirements in schools are a positive step in attempting to reduce the bullying problem, however stigma still exists regarding the discussion of psychiatric visits and mental health issues. Schools and society in general regard these diagnoses as confidential, negative and taboo. Since research clearly demonstrates psychopathology in both bullies and victims and efficacious intervention depends on appropriate diagnosis, outcomes for students who need mental health supports are expected to be poor without this discussion. Although some children are evaluated and identified by special education, many children are not referred and do not receive services. Additionally, children are often in need of diagnostic and treatment services but despite the need, mental health resources are either often not suggested or readily available. Violence permeates society and is portrayed vividly by the media on a daily basis. Not all violence is associated with bullying, but adult mental health consequences of childhood maltreatment are well documented and maltreatment by peers (i.e., bullying) have long-term adverse effects (Lereya et al. 2015).

Lessons can be learned from the tragic school shootings that have taken place. Childhood mental health issues, as they relate to characteristics of school shooters provides an interesting discussion. Shooters, many times also identified as "loners," are intriguing in that one questions whether these individuals were outliers and recognized by educators during school years as needing intervention. Chances are good that the "loner" who shot individuals in the bible study group in Charleston, South Carolina, attended school for a number of years, and was identified as "troubled." The Sandy Hook shooter from Newtown, Connecticut attended school and was recognized as needing mental health intervention. Peter Lanza is quoted as saying that his son Adam was "just a normal little weird kid." He struggled with his emotions, had poor self-esteem, was hypersensitive to physical touch, and wrote disturbing stories in 5th grade. A teacher noted he was "intelligent but not normal, with anti-social issues." As a middle school student, he avoided eye contact and developed a stiff, lumbering gait. All characteristics mentioned are consistent with Asperger syndrome, a diagnosis he received at age thirteen. At fourteen, he was taken to the Yale Child Study Center and subsequently to other mental health professionals, none of whom noted violent tendencies to harm others. Coupled with his obsession with mass murder, failing college coursework pursuits, considering himself a loner and responding only to his mother through email while sharing the same house, he planned the massacre and carried it out (Solomon 2014).

There is a strong lesson from this sad event; he was a special education student who was intelligent, with typical characteristics of Asperger syndrome, having significant needs that had been identified. The tragedy is that, if a strong system of school- and community-based mental health services were in place for the family, chances are that mental health providers would have provided a higher level of preventative care when he started having such difficulties in middle school. Disjointed efforts to take responsibility for the family with school not involved, parents divorced, the son refusing treatment and the mother challenged by escalating and serious behaviors resulted in a tragedy. Sterzing et al. (2012) suggest schools target the particular characteristics of autism spectrum disorders. It this case, early on, Adam Lanza's significant needs were not usually different from others with high functioning autism spectrum disorders. Although his actions were horrific, what can be learned from this event is that mental health delivery system and articulation with schools needs a significant overhaul.

Unfortunately, schools are challenged by students who are identified with more severe special education disabilities and are often unable to provide the level of services they need. As a result, they are often transferred to special schools outside of their communities (and often not appropriate) or placed on home instruction. School districts only meeting annually to review the student's program forget about the student. Audits indicate some states such as Georgia continue to have weak programs in serving children with behavioral disorders, segregating children in separate settings. The United States Department of Justice's Civil Rights Division revealed findings from an investigation into Georgia's program Georgia Network for Educational and Therapeutic Support, (GNETS) for students with behavioral disabilities revealing it was responsible for 'illegal segregation' of students with special needs in 'inferior facilities.' According to the Department of Justice Report, the network shunts children with the behavior problems off to the side, deprives them of educational opportunities other children have, and stigmatizes them (Shearer, 2015). Segregation of students with emotional disabilities is often an inappropriate practice, serving to place students away from appropriate peer models and rarely providing them with appropriate supports and interventions.

Additionally, some students who have emotional disabilities are not referred and evaluated by special education personnel at all, especially when they are quiet, internalizing, and do not demonstrate severe acting-out behaviors. Students who are different, do not create problems for the teacher, and "loners" are at risk for becoming victims or bully-victims; this is significant given that research demonstrates bully-victims to have the poorest outcomes compared to pure bullies or pure victims.

Unfortunately, mental health services are limited in schools. Urban schools are more likely to have articulation agreements with mental health clinics providing services on school sites, however these arrangements are uncommon. The federal IDEA is the only law in school providing services for youth identified as having a disability interfering with their ability to learn. Students with emotional issues requiring educational counseling in the school setting are not receiving the intensity of counseling services needed. Schools are underfunded by federal government and rely on local taxpayer money to supplement the many unfunded mandates. Psychiatric diagnosis and treatment is the exception rather than the rule because it is cost prohibitive for schools with limited budgets. The child psychiatrist, rarely utilized, is hired only as an outside consultant for a one-time evaluation of a child. Concerns exist because youth in need of mental health services is increasing.

Schools have instituted Positive Behavior Interventions and Supports (PBIS) systems through a tiered system, commonly known in schools as RtI. Common concerns include insufficient develop of Tiers II and III resulting in unaddressed emotional and behavioral needs for students with more complex mental health needs. Additionally, Tier I does not address broader community data and mental health prevention. The purpose of the Interconnected Systems Framework (ISF) is to integrate School Mental Health (SMH) programs and PBIS, blending educational and mental health systems and resources within a multitiered framework (Eber, Weist, and Barrett, 2013). In most states and school districts, PBIS and SMH continue to develop independently from one another resulting in a fragmented system of distrust, lack of role definition, training and watered-down evidence-based mental health services and lack of community participation. There is a need to develop "mental health literacy" and everyday strategies for promoting mental health funding sources. Shifts in procedures are necessary because schools often use ineffective practices such as out-of-school or ISS, resulting in less student time in the classroom, increased risk for students not in school and no access to mental health or behavioral support (Sugai and Stephan, 2013).

School bullying is now regarded as a very serious concern with the literature consistently demonstrating its negative effects. Lereya et al. using data from UK and U.S. longitudinal studies compared the effects of maltreatment and peer bullying on mental health outcomes in young adults. They found those bullied by peers had *worse* long-term adverse effects such as anxiety, depression, self-harm and suicidality compared to being maltreated as a child by adults. Wolfe et al. (2014) found involvement with bullying in any role is predictive of negative health, financial, behavioral, and social outcomes in adulthood and interventions in childhood are likely to reduce long-term health and social costs. These findings suggest the provision of mental health resources is essential and schools, having access to most children, are the appropriate and natural environment where school and community mental health providers can coordinate resources for children who are bullied. There is an urgent need for mental health supports and assessment teams in every school with improved integration between schools and communities to address needs of students showing signs of psychological distress (Astor et al. 2013). Data and research is needed to explore the efficacy of such interagency policies and processes in preventing bullying and victimization.

The dangers of bullying are great. Horrevorts et al. (2014) in a Dutch study examining the relationship between bullying, school climate, and psychotic experiences among adolescents revealed that both bullying and being bullied in school classes was associated with an increased level of subclinical psychotic experiences. Results from this study underscore the importance of establishing a positive school climate. Cyberbullying and mental health issues among students post significant challenges that significantly disrupt the learning process and quantity of children's lives. All students have the right to a quality education where adults help them feel wanted, valued, safe, and secure. If they are fragile, they deserve to be protected from children who use them to get the power they desperately want. Students who persistently bully need mental health services that are sustained, researched based, and integrated with their educational and home life.

Chapter 5

Bully-Victims, Victims and Students Most Vulnerable to Bullying

Bullying is difficult to stop because of the availability of smart phones with cameras, YouTube, Twitter, and apps providing effortless ways to take individuals' private behaviors and immediately make them public. Society responds in horror to incidences such as the one experienced by 68-year-old Karen Kline, a New York State school bus monitor, relentlessly taunted by three 7th grade students making fun of her weight, hearing aid, and sweat glands (Preston 2012). A cell phone, capturing the incident then posted on YouTube resulted in the outpouring of public sentiment and global outrage where in excess of $700,000 was donated to her from at least 84 countries and all 50 states in the nation. Bullying, researched in many countries around the world, is an act that has significant and far-reaching effects on students who perpetrate and students who are targets. The effects of bullying on victims have been documented worldwide. Ayernibiowo (2011) found Nigerian children to experience psychological distress including reduced self-esteem, poor physical health, decreased school attendance, and performance. Although terminology from study to study varies, much of the scientific literature refers to the bully-victim, who exhibits characteristics of pure targets and pure bullies demonstrating both anxious and aggressive behavior (Olweus 2011) while others are considered passive victims. Studies consistently suggest students who both bully and are victims (bully-victims) have the worst outcomes.

FREQUENCY OF VICTIMIZATION

Frequencies of being bullied vary due to difficulties in delineating differences between victims and bully-victims. Nansel and colleagues (2001) found 6% of their sample to be bully-victims, compared to 11% being passive victims.

According to Indicator 11 of the Indicators of School Crime and Safety survey conducted by the National Center for Educational Statistics (NCES, 2012) 28% of 12- to 18-year-old students were bullied at school, and 9% were cyberbullied during the school year. This was highest in White students, 6th-graders, public schools versus private schools, suburban versus rural schools, and occurred most frequently in hallways, stairwells, compared to classrooms. On the other hand, cyberbullying was found more frequently in female students through hurtful information on the Internet while more males were harassed while gaming. Cyberbullying was highest among White students, being in 10th grade, and in suburban areas. Students were more likely not to report cyberbullying compared to traditional forms of being bullied in school and notifying an adult was more likely to occur among students in sixth through 9th grades.

CHARACTERISTICS OF VICTIMS AND BULLY-VICTIMS

Bullying causes significant effects on the victim or as described by some researchers in more hopeful, less permanent terms, the target (Casebeer 2012). Targets are defenseless children with low social status, who are powerless in efforts to stop the bullying and have difficulty asserting them selves (Olweus 1993). They are sensitive, lonely (Nansel et al. 2001) and are deliberately, habitually, and publicly avoided. In spite of desiring friends, some students are alone all day, excluded from activities, teased or physically bullied in locker rooms, spit on, and have never been invited to birthday parties, play dates, or proms. Increased depression and anxiety as well as insomnia, nervousness, melancholy, indifference, lack of concentration and social phobias have also been observed in victims (Leymann 1990). Studies also demonstrate students socially manipulated by peers are found to have lower overall academic achievement (Morrow, Hubbard and Swift 2014).

Research suggests a genetic component may explain the involvement of children who are recipients of aggression (DiLalla and Gheyara 2014). Observations of play interactions, indicated children paired with unfamiliar same sex peers and receiving aggression were more aggressive themselves during these interactions. Findings stress the importance of utilizing social skill development and assertiveness training in young children to reduce aggression between peers. Validation, acceptance, and recognition by one's peer group are common needs of children. Being excluded and ignored is painful and very upsetting to students *and* parents. In fact, nothing is more devastating to parents than the exclusion, marginalization, and isolation of their child. Research demonstrates adolescents who are ignored puts them at risk for psychological maladjustment later on (Bowker et al. 2014).

Teachers, historically expect victimized children to either ignore or stand up to children who bully them, however they do not realize that the children lack the power, social skills, and status to do so. Studying 1,853 Canadian children, Craig, Pepler, and Blais (2007) found a significant group of students did nothing to stop bullying. Furthermore, the longer the bullying had been going on, the less effective they perceived their own strategies to stop it. Children who bully often target children who are most vulnerable, unable to defend themselves and sometimes lack expressive language skills to communicate with adults supervising them.

ASSOCIATION BETWEEN VICTIMIZATION AND MENTAL HEALTH DISORDERS

Bullying has devastating effects on its victims, including absenteeism, poor achievement, health issues, and other social problems. Studies show children who are consistently bullied by peers have an increased risk of developing new mental-health-related symptoms, and children who have high levels of mental health problems are more likely to be bullied (Fekkes et al. 2006; Salmon, James, and Smith 1998). Zwierzynska, Wolke, and Lereya (2013), conducting a longitudinal study in children from seven to ten years and again from 11 to 14 years, found children who bullied presented with emotional and depressive symptoms, and these symptoms were independent of whether bullying had been reported. Research indicates involvement in bullying either as a bully perpetrator or as a victim has been found to predict suicidal ideation (Undheim 2013). Bullied adolescents (males and females) are at risk for suicidal ideation, with additional risk if depressed. Shireen et al. (2014) found suicide attempts to be higher in girls who were perpetrators or victims.

Bullying has a demoralizing effect on society, communities, and schools. Parents are often *very* aware of who is bullying and feeling helpless when their districts are unresponsive, resort to extreme measures such as school district transfer or litigation. Frequently, vulnerable children are placed with children who bully during recess, in cafeterias, on school buses, with little regard for sufficient adult monitoring, providing ideal settings for the bully-victim dynamic. A student reports,

> I was practically 6 foot tall in the 7th grade and fairly well built as result of years of competitive swimming and a father who was a former drill instructor. I was the small one in the family. My father forbade me to fight one on one with anyone. On a bus ride home after school there was a student who stood out because he was gay and was being picked on by the school's popular bully. I remembered my father saying I had to help those in trouble and stand up for

those who couldn't stand up for themselves. Seeing this poor kid get picked on for no reason and no one doing a thing about it made me feel that I needed to take action. I intervened by placing myself (a full foot taller than the bully) between the bully and his victim. I received some punches in the face and blocked a few, and pretty much embarrassed the bully by making him look weak in front of the rest of the students on the bus. The next day in school the bully cornered me with six other students. Insults were directed at me. I said nothing because I was shy, and up until the day before, I avoided conflict because it gave me a sense of anxiety. For a full week, I was subjected to this. On the bus, the bully avoided me because he had no real support against me on the bus. In school, he would turn as many people against me as possible and always go after me in a group. I hated being in school. My very few friends became fewer and I felt that I could talk to no one. Teachers had a hard time believing me because my older brother was such a brawler and I was the biggest kid in the grade. How could he have a bullying problem? After school on a Friday, I was walking to a friend's house and was confronted by the bully and the same six kids from the other day. I was knocked to the ground and held down by all the kids, one on each arm and two on each leg. The bully then lit a cigarette and proceeded to put it out on my right arm. He relit the cigarette and put it out on my left arm. He did this two more times. I never told my parents and hid the marks with long sleeve shirts. In school, the harassment continued for another year. I dealt with this by hiding myself and refused to take the bus because I was afraid of more confrontation. Eventually my father's job moved us out of state and I started at a new high school. Years later I returned to my old town with the intent on revenge (I was on the wrestling team now at my new high school). I found the six students and the bully. The bully was in jail along with three of the kids who developed drug problems. I could see their lives were going to be much worse than the beating I wanted to give them. I haven't been back to that town in a long time. I still have the scars, but they are only on the outside.

STUDENTS WITH DISABILITIES WHO ARE BULLIED

Students with disabilities are vulnerable to bullying because they frequently present with delays in social and communication skills and appear different. Blake et al. (2012) examined prevalence rates of bullying and risk for repeated victimization among students with disabilities finding 24.5% of elementary and 34.1% middle school children with disabilities were bullied, one and half times the national average for students without disabilities. Students with emotional disabilities and autism spectrum disorders were at the greatest risk of experiencing victimization, with peak rates during the middle school years. Furthermore, students with disabilities who were bullied once were at high risk of being bullied repeatedly.

Research demonstrates students with disabilities may be victimized more because they are passive, misread nonverbal communication, and misinterpret non-threatening cues. Some lack the social skills necessary to avoid victimization, and in some cases develop aggressive characteristics resulting from prolonged victimization (Rose et al. 2011). Son et al. (2014) examined risk and protective factors of peer victimization among students with language delays and found they are also at risk. Studying child, family, and school characteristics at one point and then peer socialization two years later, pre-elementary children with disabilities attending special education programs, having lower socioeconomic status, and lower receptive language are found to be most at risk. A teacher shares her experience in the classroom:

> A current student of mine is bullied without his knowledge. His auditory processing time is so severely delayed, the moment has come and passed before he can even understand what was being said or done to him. Furthermore, he is unable to defend himself because he doesn't have the cognitive ability to retaliate. This leads to my frustration and the breakdown of the educational goals created for him.

Frequently, students with disabilities endure years of victimization in school, and are subjected to ridicule and taunting because they are vulnerable and easily manipulated, resulting in the development of psychosocial issues that are detrimental to their overall psychological being, and feelings of being unpopular, unhappy, and unsafe at school (Mishna 2003).

STUDENTS WITH AUTISM SPECTRUM DISORDERS WHO ARE BULLIED

Students with autism spectrum disorders (ASD) are especially vulnerable to victimization in elementary school (Chen and Schwartz 2012) and during adolescence. Sterzing et al. (2012) examining prevalence and correlates of bullying involvement among adolescents with ASD found 46.3% to be victimized with correlates being White non-Hispanic, having ASD and ADHD, poor social skills and poor conversational ability. Those with better social skills were less likely to experience victimization and those with more conversational abilities, in inclusive settings, and having a diagnosis of ADHD were more likely to be bullied.

Studying 192 children with autism, 77% of parents reported their child had been bullied within the last month and 30% reported victimization two or more times per week (Cappadocia, Weiss, and Pepler 2011). Factors associated with being bullied included age, internalizing, and externalizing mental health problems, communication difficulties, number of friends at school, and parent's mental health problems.

Students with high functioning autism spectrum disorders (Asperger's disorder under the former DSM-IV) are especially vulnerable to bullying (Kloosterman et al. 2013). Parents reported 94% of their children with high functioning autism spectrum disorders (HFASD) victimized (Little 2002) while Carter (2005) found 65% bullied, with nearly 50% afraid of peers, and 33% never invited to birthday parties. Students with HFASD often have social communication disabilities with average to above intelligence, placing them in general education classes, often without special education supports. Unable to read social cues, presenting with lack of tact, pedantic in expression, and often brutally honest, it is difficult for even the most tolerant peers, not understanding the disability, to know how to respond. Asperger (1944) the Austrian pediatrician after whom the disorder was named, reported the incessant tormenting and teasing by peers, not markedly different from what is demonstrated in schools seventy years later. Students with ASD who have a very naïve understanding of social situations are placed into the same classes with children who persistently bully and manipulate others to gain the power and status they need. Being so different, and so vulnerable, this student is the perfect victim (Klin, Volkmar, and Sparrow 2000).

Bullying of students with ASD results in them having long-lasting effects of internalizing problems such as attention problems in younger children, and depression in adolescents (Ghuzuiddin, Weidmer-Mikhail and Ghazuiddin 1998). Additionally, 20% of adolescents and young adults with HFASD met criteria for major depressive disorder, 30% demonstrated generalized anxiety disorder, and 50% had clinically significant levels of suicidal ideation (Shatayermman et al. 2007). Sadly, higher functioning students on the spectrum want friends, but lack skills to develop relationships. One parent reported her child wanted to be put in the street and run over to end the pain of being bullying. Another child was egged on to "run like a bull," laughed at and called "freak". Students with ASD are physically awkward, socially naïve, eccentric in nature, and struggle to understand why they are not liked. Sadly, as one parent shared, she felt wounded when seeing her child excluded and treated as a peripheral person (Carter 2009). A middle school girl reported she was taunted and bullied by a student for years while the school did nothing to stop it:

> I'm very stressed with school because boys are bothering me and I can't find a good way to stop them. I tell the office people and my parents but they find a new way to torture me every day and I have had enough. My mother wrote a letter to the superintendent, but he didn't do anything and it's been going on for years.

Girls with ASD are especially vulnerable because they often receive a late diagnosis, and do not receive school supports during their early school years. Girls on the spectrum have a difficult time surviving socially complicated female interactions and exclusion by peers. Experiences of women with ASD are frequently characterized by a profound sense of alienation, fear, and being invisible (Wiley 1999).

Educators need to plan interventions for middle school students with high functioning ASD's when hormonal changes coupled with sensory overload and fascination with special interests can take a dangerous turn. Both males and females have obsessional interests in things including horses, trains, colors, vacuum cleaners, guns, other weapons, World Wars, anime, and computer games, and may be driven to inappropriately engage with that interest. Baron-Cohen (2000) suggested that the special interest is a difference in cognitive style, where a child is immersed in a world of things rather than people. Unfortunately, this interest can be a hindrance because the preoccupation interferes with normal development because the individual refuses to learn about anything outside of it. Although violence is usually not associated with ASD's, and individuals are often victims and rule-bound, an all-consuming special interest can result in poor judgment and involvement with local law enforcement. In New York State, a male with an ASD having extensive knowledge and interest in transportation was jailed 29 times for stealing buses and trains.

Strong powerful interests played a part in the Sandy Hook Elementary School massacre in Newtown, Connecticut. Adam Lanza was diagnosed with Asperger syndrome, obsessive-compulsive disorder, significant social and language delays, had special interests in war, guns, and computer games, an awkward gate, and little eye contact. He was incredibly sad, isolated, and intelligent (Solomon 2014). He had significant educational and mental health challenges, was obsessed with and owned guns, accumulated extensive data on mass shootings especially Columbine, refused medication, and mental health supports (State of Connecticut Department of Criminal Justice, 2013). Although it will never be known if the extreme violent behaviors demonstrated were due to being bullied in school, the tragedy illustrates the complexities, challenges and failures of the parents, educational, and mental health systems to coordinate services and respond to the needs of this troubled individual. Each of these entities needs to know how to access supports when an individual is acknowledged to have significant mental health disturbances. Adolescents with ASD are uniquely vulnerable to bullying given their social skill deficits that are hallmarks of the condition (Sterzing et al. 2012). Anti-bullying programs should incorporate interventions that address the core deficit of ASD while educating peers about the condition.

BULLYING BASED ON RELIGION OR RACE

Research exploring bullying based on religious differences is scarce. Students sometimes target peers because of the religious symbols worn. For example, Muslim girls' hijabs (head scarves), Sikh boys' patka or dastaar (turbans), and Jewish boys' yarmulkes are sometimes removed by others and thrown around buses or classrooms. Over the past decade, there has been a rise in anti-Muslim and anti-Sikh bullying that may have roots in a perceived association of religious heritage and terrorism (New York State Education Department, DASA). A student reports,

> I can remember the television movie, The Holocaust, with Meryl Streep. Before the movie was on, my grandfather told me if anyone ever made fun of me for being Jewish, don't let them see you cry. I did not understand what he was talking about. After the movie, many of the kids in my class were acting out the movie as the Nazis. They made up armbands with swastikas. As I am writing this, I wonder where the teacher was and the parents of the bullies because they were making the armbands up at home and in class. The teacher had to see them with the bands on and doing the Nazi salute. Their plan was to chase me around the playground along with a few other kids they put on the "Jewish Team." Instead of going outside, I got in trouble in the lunchroom so I went straight to detention. Apparently, they carried out their plan on the playground chasing and beating up the kids on the "Jewish Team." They had so much fun that they planned to do it the next day. Not wanting to go outside I made believe that I had a headache and went to the nurse's office. However, the second attack was not successful. A kid that I played baseball with ripped up the Nazi armbands and beat up the leader. I can remember him telling me what happened in front of the library. Now, as an adult I thought about how this incident impacted me throughout my childhood and into adulthood. I am very quick to point out that I am Jewish because I believe I am disarming the people around me and letting them know that they should not say anything anti-Semitic. As for the bully making up the armbands, he was a friend of mine; that lasted for another year and then ended because he moved. I now understand what my grandfather tried to tell me.

Students are also bullied based on race. One teacher shares her story:

Growing up I never personally experienced bullying. I grew up in the city where everyone is so diverse that I never understood what "minority" meant until I went to college and was one of about thirty Hispanics in the entire school along with fourteen African Americans and six Asian students. During that time, I used to work as a waitress at a restaurant where I felt what it was like to be seen as a minority for the first time. I was treated by some customers as inferior because I was Hispanic and waiting on their table. Their comments would include, "You're not American are you?" I felt like replying, if you are referring to the United States of America, yes I am American because I was born in New York. If you are inquiring about my nationality, my parents are from Colombia. The most ignorant question was "Are you Mexican?" Did I ever complain or mention it to my superiors? In four years, I did only once, and that person was removed from the establishment. So, I can relate to kids not wanting to speak up. In my case I did not want to cause issues for the place where I worked, I needed my job, so I would just suck it in and smile. These people were ADULTS! If this is how the adults behave, then is this what we can expect from their offspring? At 17 years old, my parents gave me a strong foundation and I had not experienced this type of situation before but it is definitely engraved in my memory. Because of my experience, now I purposely make sure I do not do anything that would fall under a "spic" stereotype. Had I gone through this type of racial harassment while a child I am not sure what the lasting consequences would have been. Now that my daughters are in school, I worry if they will have to deal with the ignorance of others. All I can do is guide them to be confident and stand up for themselves.

LESBIAN, GAY, BISEXUAL, AND TRANSGENDERED (LGBT) VICTIMIZATION

Gendered harassment, described as including any unwanted behavior that enforces traditional, heterosexual gender norms including sexual harassment, homophobic, biphobic, or transphobic harassment, and harassment for gender-nonconformity (Meyer 2008, 25) is a significant problem in schools. Students who are LGBT experience more bullying and sexual harassment (79%) than heterosexual students (50%), (Coker, Austin, and Schuster 2010). The significant vulnerability of this population to victimization and harassment needs special attention in schools, because outcomes for students who are LGBT experiencing bullying are poor.

Effects of bullying and harassment include missed school days due to fear of peers and increased likeliness of considering or attempting suicide. Poteat et al. (2011) researching homophobic victimization and its effects on school belonging in LGBT and heterosexual White youth adolescents found those who experienced victimization reported feeling a lower sense of school belonging, more frequently skipped school, had poorer academic performance, and felt it was less important to graduate. In this study, parent support had no effect on suicidality and school belonging in LGBT youth, suggesting school psychologists actively work with parents to assist with supporting their victimized children.

Research indicates outcomes are poor also for LGBT adults because they recall experiences of victimization in school influencing them later in life. Greene, Britton, and Fitts (2014) found school-related peer bullying was predictive of fear of negative evaluation later in adulthood. Results imply that counseling for LGBT youth include empowerment and increasing self-esteem. Pritchard (2013) investigating the identification and safety in a sample of LGBT African American students argues that current measures to keep them safe in school fail. The research calls attention to the large number of bias-motivated suicides in this population. They experience a triple whammy due to this "tri-cultural experience" facing homophobia, racism, and exclusion from their own ethnic groups. Pritchard argues adults are complicit in youth bullying because of their own bias hidden in established school policy and should be held accountable.

Another reason for high rates of bullying in the LGBT population is because teachers are less likely to intervene in harassment related to sexual orientation, gender presentation and body size compared to other forms of bias including race, religion, and disability (California Safe Schools Coalition 2004). A recent National Education Association survey found teachers and education support professionals expressed a need for more training on bully prevention related to students' sexual orientation, gender issues, and racial issues (Bradshaw et al. 2013). Payne and Smith (2012) argue schools need to adopt an alternate framework to understand bullying among LGBT students because schools persistently privilege specific groups of youth while marginalizing others. Schools are places where normative gender and sexuality are privileged and this perception functions as a tool to target peers.

FEMALES STUDENTS WHO ARE BULLIED

Research indicates females bully both verbally and nonverbally in efforts to gain peer group status. Female victims sometimes resort to plastic surgery to avoid being bullied (Jane 2014) and many report being bullied because they were overweight. This phenomenon was recently studied in the Netherlands by Jansen et al. (2014) investigating the association between body mass index (BMI), and bullying involvement among young children (mean age = 6.2 years). A higher BMI was associated with increased victimization and bullying perpetration. Although results are not surprising, what is surprising is the relatively young average age of the sample bullying peers.

One female student shares the devastating effects of being bullied for being overweight:

As a former victim of bullying, I know first-hand what kind of damage harassment and discrimination can do to a child. It started in about 5th and lasted until I was in 9th grade. It was mainly one boy and one girl leading the bullying and sometimes their friends would join in. They bullied me because I was overweight and I never said anything about it. The one time I mentioned to my school counselor that I wanted to change my class because one girl was picking on me a lot, but she brushed me off. As a kid, I thought that if I'm truthful, and the adults who are supposed to be in charge do nothing about it, why would I tell them? That's why it's important for teachers to take these things very seriously. I even tried to befriend my bullies. I went to a sleepover they invited me to and for the most part, I just ended up being made fun of. I would also let them borrow money, or a pencil if they didn't have one. I thought that this would make them see that I was a nice person, and they didn't have to make fun of me. Unfortunately, that was not the case. I ended up with a lot of social anxiety because of the emotional distress they put me through every day. The bullying only lasted until 9th grade because I didn't want to go to school anymore. I transferred to another school and was nervous to meet new people, figuring there would just be a new crop of bullies to pick on me. I didn't know how else to express my emotional distress other than by manifesting physical symptoms. People don't quite understand when you tell them you're anxious and hurting inside, understanding only physical pain. I told my Mom that I was getting migraine headaches every day and I couldn't go to school. I ended up on home tutoring and finished my high school years at home. I missed out on a lot because these few people had such an impact on me. They drove me away and that is very unfortunate.

Bullying negatively impacts educational outcomes such as academic self-efficacy and educational achievement in females (Popp et al. 2014), however findings indicate they can be protected by at least having one friend (Cardoos and Hisshaw 2011). Bullying can also erode self-esteem, as another female shares:

I have personally experienced this type of bullying in my own life. In middle school, I was overweight for my age. It wasn't so much what I was eating or the fact that I wasn't exercising, but more of my body's reaction to adolescence. Regardless of the reason why I was overweight, I quickly learned how bullying could affect someone's young life, and demolish any sense of security or self-esteem. Going to recess was a nightmare and a time that I dreaded. A certain group of three students would constantly verbally torment me. Rather than include me in their sports games, they would throw the ball or kick it away from me. They would say things like "you're too fat to get it in time" or things like "you should have been able to stop it with your size." I would try to laugh these things off and act like I thought they were just as funny as the bullies thought they were. But I would go home crying, I was unsure of why I wasn't good enough or would ask myself why I couldn't be like the "normal" kids. My situation took a turn for the worse on my 8th grade picture day. I had gone out the weekend before and picked out an outfit with my mom that made me feel beautiful. I was so excited to show up to school in it, and was sure, this would be the day I would fit in. The outfit was similar to those of the "cool kids." It wasn't baggy, but more clean cut. I showed up to school that day with my hair done and pulled back, smiling and excited to boast this new outfit. (A new outfit seems like such a small deal, but it was the thought of fitting in that made it so wonderful). The morning passed and it was time for recess. I walked outside more confident than I had been in years. However, my positive attitude and streak of confidence was crushed just as quickly as I had acquired it. The leader of the three bullies looked at me as I walked outside and said, "Why didn't you think to buy a girdle with that outfit?" It was the first time I couldn't hide my emotions or my feelings. I burst into tears and ran off the playground. This was this moment that triggered my five year struggle with an eating disorder to be physically unhealthily thin and pretty. It wasn't until my second year of college that I acquired the help that I needed to realize that my beauty did not lie in my physical appearance, and that the eating disorder was not helping me but rather, was making me sick and slowly killing me. I look back on that time as one of the darkest times of my life. Those bullies did hold power over me. No, they did not physically abuse me, but in my opinion, that would have been better than what they did do. They took away my self-confidence and self-esteem that took me years to regain. At the time of this bullying, no teacher, administrator, or staff member could see what was happening.

VULNERABILITY BECAUSE THEY ARE JUST DIFFERENT

Essentially, any difference makes students vulnerable to bullying. Children with food allergies are at risk just because they are different and may need certain accommodations such as sitting at a chemical-free table at lunch. One parent shares, "My son has severe food allergies, and we've been lucky so far in his school because he hasn't had a problem with the kids bullying him. But, I'm hearing of children who will wave something like a peanut butter sandwich under the nose of a child who has an allergy to it. Children can be very cruel." Children who have acne are also at risk:

> When it comes to bullying it hits home. One of my cousins was bullied when he was in middle school and part of high school. He had a bad case of acne, and he tried different medications but nothing worked. He finally convinced my aunt to put him on this one type of medication that was so powerful, that he needed to see the doctor monthly to get his liver checked. The reason he wanted to get on this risky drug was because he was getting bullied at school. The name he was called made me sick to my stomach. I couldn't believe that kids would be so mean and cruel, all for a few laughs. Making someone feel so useless is horrible. I could only imagine how he felt.

HEALTH OUTCOMES OF VICTIMS

Research consistently demonstrates being bullied is linked to poor outcomes including internalizing symptoms among students and lasting effects into adulthood. Wolke et al. (2013) studied bullying effects in childhood on adult health, wealth, crime, and social relationships finding bullying in any role had negative effects on health and wealth and social functioning. This was especially true for those chronically victimized by peers.

Copeland et al. (2014) found victims bullied in childhood had more systemic low-grade systemic inflammation compared to children who were uninvolved. Conducting a longitudinal study on victims in order to predict if bullying perpetration and victimization in elementary school was associated with psychotic experiences (hallucinations, delusions) in late adolescence, Wolke et al. (2014) found an association between any type of bullying behavior and psychotic experiences at age 18. Bully-victims consistent with other studies were found to have the greatest risk for poor outcomes later in life.

Research suggests early trauma in childhood predicts internalizing problems later in life. A longitudinal study (Zwierzynska, Wolke, and Lereya 2013) collecting data during childhood and later in early adolescence found a relationship between victimization and emotional and depressive symptoms later on with increased likelihood of scoring in the severe range of these symptoms. Similar studies also agree with these findings.

A national survey conducted in the Netherlands (Idsoe, Dyregrov, and Idsoe, 2012) investigating a possible relationship between bullying and post-traumatic stress disorder (PTSD) symptoms found for all bullied students, 27.6% of the boys and 40.5% of the girls had scores with the clinical range. Correlations are found between PTSD among elementary school children who have been bullied, with symptoms including loss of concentration, increased distress and worry, jumpiness, misbehavior, physical complaints, listlessness, and extreme emotional reactions (National Child Traumatic Stress Network Schools Committee 2008).

Toxic stress and involvement in a horrifying event have also been linked to psychological distress in children including trouble sleeping, intrusive thoughts about the incident, mood swings and in some cases, PTSD. Events such as Sandy Hook in Connecticut are profoundly traumatizing for parents and the community. Children who do the best are able to integrate the experience allowing it to be an experience that is part of their lives, but not defining it as they grow, change and return to their developmental tasks. "One of the most important things is to get back on the horse" (Berkowitz, as cited in Worley, 2015, p. 10). Research reveals that youth who had a caring and supportive adult in their lives and who are supported after a traumatic event were less likely to develop psychological issues. The goal of intervention is to improve communication between an affected child and his or her caregivers, building resilience (Worley, 2015, p. 13). Findings from this study can be applied to events such as bullying, often a stressful and traumatic event. If there is a teacher or a caregiver who is caring and supportive, the child is less likely to suffer from psychological distress. Unfortunately, children who are victimized often feel they have no one to turn to.

ADULTS WHO ARE VICTIMS

Teachers are not immune from bullying, being threatened, physically and verbally abused and are sometimes afraid of students who persistently and chronically bully. Eighty percent of teachers report at least one victimization experience in the current or past year, and of those who experience an offense, 94% report being victimized by students (McMahon et al. 2011). This suggests that school changes include increased administrator awareness of staff safety and policies that train personnel (Espelage et al. 2013). In 2006, when state lawmakers enacted the Workplace Violence Prevention Act (Frenett 2014) to develop and implement programs to prevent and minimize workplace violence and help ensure the safety of public employees, protected were employees from state agencies, fire departments, school safely agents of the New York Police Department and public authorities and political subdivisions of the state. Those excluded include public school district and county vocational education employees. Unfortunately, in States like New York, laws do not protect adults in schools from workplace violence and students who bully them, placing the responsibility on school districts to develop appropriate codes of conduct.

CONCLUSIONS

Research indicates persistent victimization of any type has negative long-term academic, physiological, and psychological effects on students and their families. Parents frequently and out of desperation, resort to moving in order to transfer their child to another school as illustrated:

> The most appalling situation that I came across was when a friend in middle school was being bullied to the point where she would no longer come to school. Between periods, this group of girls would seek her out and physically and emotionally assault her. I remember she had chunks of hair missing from her head because of the abuse. I never witnessed the bullying first hand but other students did and they were all too scared to help her and stand up for her. It got to the

point where she had to leave our district and finish her schooling elsewhere. This was completely unfair and sad. Faculty and administrators were not taking the situation seriously enough and were not provided with tools to resolve the conflict. The parents finally moved and she started at a new school.

The vulnerability of students with disabilities and those who are LGBT warrant the need for proactive supports, especially in unstructured and unsupervised settings and on social media. Children are increasingly exposed to violent, traumatic events and experience toxic stress, from being bullied in some cases throughout their entire school careers. Without educators and parents acting as social guardians and significant efforts to change the behaviors of those who persistently bully them, their prognosis is slim. Without significant efforts to provide caring and supportive educators who are available to *be there*, bullied children will have poor outcomes in life.

Chapter 6

Implications for Schools

Practices for Consideration and Future Research

Educators, mental health providers, pediatricians, and parents need to be more proactive in utilizing interventions for bullying. Schools provide optimal opportunities for students to dominate others in order to achieve desirable social status and power. Students who persistently bully in school despite intervention are predicted to have negative outcomes later in life and need immediate and long-term intervention. Research demonstrates bullying serves to maintain and raise power, social status, and prestige, therefore interventions should focus on finding socially appropriate replacement alternatives to enable the student to fulfill the same need.

Schools need to take a strong stance for successful behavioral change recognizing that previous attempts are likely to be misdirected, disjointed, generic, and not research based. School administrators and school boards should become change agents, using research to drive practice, finding creative ways to access mental health resources where students at risk can receive treatment early. "Linkage between research and practice is the answer to the question of how to eradicate bullying among youth" (Swearer et al. 2010, 43).

Bullying prevention is the best course of action, but good prevention is slow to evolve, and expensive. Realistically, and unfortunately, litigation resulting from newly mandated state bullying and harassment laws will force certain aspects of change to take place, especially when bullying constitutes discrimination infringing on students' civil rights. Ideally, considering research findings offers numerous suggestions for practice in schools and the means to avoid litigation.

PAYING ATTENTION TO PREDICTORS AND
RISK FACTORS AMONG STUDENTS

Research suggests educators and parents pay attention to certain risk factors and characteristics among children who bully, and be proactively responsive to them, because outcomes are poor. Children either nominated through surveys or not responding to customary behavioral interventions may need intense, long-term, and aggressive treatment. Research demonstrates children at risk are those who also have a combination of ADHD, ODD, and CD with a small percentage also having CU traits. A meta-analysis of behavioral treatments for students with ADHD demonstrates consistent evidence that behavioral treatments are effective for treating ADHD (Fabiano et al. 2009) and adolescents with CU traits may respond to functional family therapy (White et al. 2013).

Popular students including cheerleaders and athletes may be students who bully. Parent conflict is also positively related to bullying others (Hemphill et al. 2012; Georgious and Stavrinides 2013) therefore, educators need to be cognizant that parent conflict may predict the manifestation of bullying in school. If investigating a situation, educators need to be careful about not suspending the victim, who may be retaliating against the student who bullies. Outcomes for this student (the bully-victim) are significantly worse compared to outcomes of children who bully or children who are victims. Gender also needs to be considered because females and males perpetrate differently and evidence suggests both are equally likely to cyberbully peers.

COUNSELING FOR STUDENTS WHO BULLY

Enactment of new State anti-bullying and harassment legislation requires schools to provide counseling for children who bully, however specific strategies and frequencies of treatment are not well defined leaving decisions to schools and psychologists. Schools need *specific* protocols to identify bullying, and *specific* interventions to change the child's bullying behavior. Each child engaging in bullying behavior needs an individualized plan that may include checking in with the student, teachers and parents several times a day. Examining reports of children who were bullies and bully-victims, Farrington and Baldry (2010) suggest these children may benefit from the use of cognitive behavior skills training.

Counselors and teachers need to understand the needs and motivations of the child who bullies. Children who bully are organized, purposeful, and have a pre-mediated means of personal gain, exerting control with verbal proficiency and developed argumentative skills defending their behavior

(McAdams and Schmidt 2007). Often the bullying incident is planned to maximize gain and minimize consequences. Students who bully may patronize students and adults while disingenuously saying exactly what others want to hear (Coloroso 2002) or are grandiose and psychologically defensive (Salmivalli et al. 1999). McAdams and Schmidt (2007) suggest counselors and teachers need to avoid becoming victims themselves, using consequences of noncompliance with behavioral expectations that act as a significant deterrent to future aggressive acts. Arguments and debates should be avoided with no form of compromise and variable response protocols should be used in order to keep students uncertain about the specific consequences of their behaviors. Counselors and teachers should reinforce positive achievements cautiously, with the exception of pro-social behaviors. Additionally, teachers must be vigilant especially in unsupervised settings maintaining an "air of suspicion," convincing the child it is their best interests to change their behavior (McAdams and Schmidt 2007). Administrators investigating bullying events should collect evidence from victims prior to confronting the child who bullies, avoiding inquiry of the child's version of events because he/she will not be truthful. Presenting students with concrete evidence, using a non-nonsense approach, avoiding long discussions while affirming the student's strengths, popularity (Crothers and Kolbert 2008) and high social status (Graham and Juvonen 1998) may have positive effects. Children who bully need direction on how to demonstrate pro-social behaviors and should receive carefully planned consequences that serve to attain the control, status, and dominance they seek. Interestingly, Claire, Poskiparta, and Salmivalli (2014) examining the efficacy of the KiVa Anti-bullying program in children from grades 1 to 9, studied the effectiveness of using a confronting (confrontational) or a nonconfronting (nonconfrontational) approach while addressing students who bully. Neither approach was effective in instances of long-term bullying.

Rigby (2012) suggests examining the desires and motivations of children who bully to support effective intervention. Children admit to bullying for different reasons, feeling justified because they are aggrieved and want to retaliate, for its entertainment value, to gain or retain group status, or acquire something. Changing children's desires by helping them develop positive relationships with classmates and use of non-punitive measures may reduce bullying.

TRAINING FOR EDUCATORS

Even with new state anti-bullying mandates for training, schools need to be vigilant with ongoing professional development in all areas of bully prevention. All teachers, especially preschool teachers, need explicit train-ing on the characteristics and risk factors commonly seen among children who chronically bully. Adopting a developmental psychopathology approach where psychological and behavioral dysfunction occurring in common child-hood psychiatric disorders is taught serves to improve teachers' understand-ing allowing them to be instrumental in referral and intervention processes. Behavioral service providers, psychologists, and special education teachers, need to work diligently with parents in analyzing their children's behaviors and determining the appropriate supports. Indicators and risk factors in young children that exist and predict problem behavior suggests schools develop early screening tools for emotional behavioral disorders (EBD) including questions for parents to report on their child's play with toys, interactions with their children, and maternal depression (Nelson et al. 2007).

Young children have complete trust in teachers to keep them safe and out of harms way. Parents also, expect teachers to have skills to protect their children while in school (in loco parentis). The tragedy is, children soon realize the adults who they thought would keep them safe, do not. An inter-view between a father and his 2nd grade son demonstrates the perception of trust:

Q. What is bullying?

Answer: Bullying is when people are mean to someone and they are not treating other people fairly. Bullies do not treat other people nicely when other people treat them nicely.

Q. Why do some kids bully?

Answer: Kids bully when they want to show off or they think bullying is cool. Some kids bully because they are asking for help through bullying.

Q. How do you stand up to a bully?

Answer: You speak firmly and say, "Stop it. I do not like it. And cut out this behavior." If they continue bullying, tell the teacher what is happening. The teacher will fix it.

Q. How would you react if someone bullies you physically?

Answer: I would free myself and run to the nearest adult I can trust.

Q. How are you different from bullies?

Answer: I help people when they need help and I am kind hearted. The bullies are not kind hearted and they do stuff that makes people sad or mad.

Q. Why do you not bully others in the school?

Answer: If I bully others, I feel bad about me for causing trouble for them.

Q. What do you do when you see someone bullies your friend?

Answer: I go tell the bully to stop it and tell the adult I can trust what happened.

Q. Do you think a student can bully a teacher?

Answer: No I do not think so because a teacher has more control of the class. And students know that if they bully a teacher, lots of trouble is waiting for them.

Q. Have you seen a teacher bullying a student?

Answer: No I have not. However, a teacher can bully a student by discouraging the student or talking down on students.

Q. Have you seen any bully? Why?

Answer: No. Because they know if they act like a bully lot of trouble is waiting for them. For example, they will have to go to principal or their parents will be called to see the teacher.

Sadly, as the years go by, students do lose hope and by high school, students are even less certain of teachers' ability to curtail bullying (Luxenburg, Limber and Olweus, 2014).

INCREASED ADULT SUPERVISION

Research suggests increasing adult supervision in unstructured settings reduces behaviors of children who bully. Paraeducators, custodians, bus drivers, school playground monitors, and special education aides, need training on bully prevention and their roles clarified on prevention, intervening with students, and reporting. Bradshaw et al. (2013) found teacher and support professionals expressed a need to include *all* members of school staff in training. Even students interviewed indicated that clearer rules, more staff supervision in hallways, and preventing and fixing the problem instead of using suspension and expulsion were needed to combat bullying (Ferrans and Silman 2014). Teacher and paraeducator supports were perceived to influence students' decisions to join bully perpetrators or not. Unfortunately, schools put educational support personnel, who are the least trained in environments highly conducive to bullying, such as hallways, stairwells, and school buses. School initiatives designed to combat bullying in unstructured settings need to be more intense because research shows bullying occurs more frequently on school buses compared to classrooms. Students who persistently bully should *not* be on the bus, requiring parents and schools to find alternative transportation. Training drivers and bus monitors who are often contracted by school districts and providing addition personnel on buses is essential to reduce bullying.

School locker rooms are concerning for students already vulnerable and significantly at risk for bullying. Requiring them to change clothes and shower for physical education classes makes them more vulnerable. One student with an autism spectrum disorder solved the problem and decided to change her clothes in the school hallway where there were adults in order to avoid the incessant torment! Providing students with access to private bathrooms or the nurses office is an obvious solution.

EXEMPLARY PRINCIPAL LEADERSHIP PRACTICES: IMPROVING SCHOOL CLIMATE

Extinguishing school bullying begins with successful principal leadership practices. School leaders who are successful in motivating and collegially working with faculty, staff, parents and students have established the necessary first step toward creating a safe environment conducive to student learning. Fortunate are students attending this type of school because they have a better chance of escaping the devastating effects of bullying because of high expectations for collegiality and trust among teachers, students, and parents. Unfortunately, many practicing teachers experience situations where administrators are informed specifically of a bullying incident in a timely manner however the follow-up on the administrator's end was never consistent, creating a negative, distrusting, and discouraging atmosphere. If teachers and staff report and perceive that nothing is ever done to address the problem, why bother? Sending this negative message perpetrates a culture of distrust and apathy instead of consistently following through with planned consequences, essential to the success of any program.

Principals, school boards, and their attorneys need to reconsider the use of ineffective strategies of suspension and expulsion and other forms of negative punishment. A recent study in New Zealand found that principals were suspending students who were victims rather than students who were caught bullying (Towl 2014). Often the victim lashes out in retaliation, and gets caught, not having the finesse of the child who bullies. Districts also need to exercise caution in adopting certain programs such as conflict resolution and peer mediation because these exacerbate bullying behavior, providing the child who bullies a forum to exercise power (Greene 2003). Children who bully are extraordinarily eloquent in denying their bullying behavior, diverting blame to others, and making others responsible. Teachers and counselors need to ensure that when groups of children are put together the groups are not vastly different in their power status (Vaillancourt, Hymel and McCougall, 2003).

School-wide positive behavioral support (SWPBS) is a framework consisting of continuum of behavioral supports. Essentially, it is a strong system of RtI ranging from universal, primary supports for all students to tertiary or intensive assistance for those not responsive. Continual provision of supports with data collection reflecting progress, or the lack of, focuses on appropriate desired behaviors. Children who persistently and chronically bully others generally need tertiary or intensive supports. Focusing on what the child who bullies does, replaces blame with a behavioral plan with positive reinforcement for pro-social behaviors and alternatives to aggression. Principals who understand the urgency of needed supports can assist in stopping some of most aggressive forms of bullying before it spirals out of control.

School leaders need to be wary of quick fix anti-bullying curricula that may have limited effectiveness, search for grants to train staff and parents, and harness seamless supports with law enforcement, psychiatrists, pediatricians and mental health agencies in the community. Furthermore, principals need to utilize surveys to establish baselines of the extent of bullying in their schools, then chart progress of anti-bullying initiatives.

PEER NOMINATION

Bullying is often a covert activity, difficult to detect, and more serious and difficult to prevent the longer it continues. It goes unnoticed with 30% of elementary and middle school students reporting being bullied in the classroom without any form of teacher intervention (Whitney and Smith 1993). Also, schools often rely on self-report surveys to measure bullying, however they are unreliable because students who bully deny their behavior and insist they are just having fun (Salmivalli, Karhunen, and Lagerspetz 1996). Children who bully are more likely to endorse attitudes justifying the use of aggression and minimizing its effect on the victims. Typically and ineffectively, many teachers expect the child who bullies to admit doing it, then has him shake hands and apologize to the child he has just bullied. Peer nomination, where students write down names of classmates who match a descriptive statement has been found to have strong concurrent and predictive validity (Leff, Power, and Goldstein 2004). Results from surveys are used to further investigate children who are nominated then result in proactive intervention and preventative counseling. Cole, Cornell and Sheras (2006) comparing the use of peer nomination versus self-report in middle school students found that peer nomination surveys identified many more students than did student self-report.

Peer-nominated children who bully are found to be a high-risk group receiving many disciplinary referrals. They are six times as likely to be suspended from school as children who do not bully and three times as likely to receive detention. Using results from peer nomination during early school years can assist with preventative counseling and other proactive interventions.

WORKING WITH PARENTS: PROBLEMS AND PROTECTIVE EFFECTS

Higher education accreditation agencies establish standards by which teacher candidates are measured for effectiveness in the field. College coursework, syllabi, and student assessments must align with these standards. The newest standards now include assessments of teacher competency on the effectiveness in their ability to engage and collaborate with families. Updated editions of textbooks are also including a chapter devoted to communication and collaboration with families. Although some progress has been made in teacher-parent collaboration, there *are very few* new procedures in place significantly different than what has always been done. Policies and teacher contracts need to change to align with these standards. Improved parent communication and collaboration may significantly improve student behavior and reduce the bullying problem.

Effective communication and strong relationships with families have shown to have a protective effect on bullying. Logically when an educator establishes open lines of communication, and has healthy relationships with parents, trust is built. Educating children and promoting acceptable behavior is not easy for teachers or parents and working together can foster confidence and consistency. Effective behavior management, including management of bullying or victimization behaviors and the sharing of ideas is invaluable. This is of paramount importance when a teacher has a difficult, maybe aggressive parent, who is uninvolved, detached, has mental health needs, and possibly demonstrates bullying behaviors themselves. Teachers will need help from principals and psychologists as well as community-based supports, and with these, can help the child's parent and in turn, the child. Teachers should have strategies in place to build resilience in parents and involvement in their schools and classrooms. Working with a parent of a child who persistently bullies may involve daily phone calls over a period of months. Calling any parent once a month with a positive comment about their child, spending 10% of the time talking about the past, and 90% taking about making things better (Fallon, 2012) can result in changing attitudes and behaviors in children and their parents. Research consistently indicates good parent-school relationships correlate with increased student achievement and reduction in both traditional and cyberbullying. Unfortunately, when there are problems with children's behavior, communication is often minimal and relationships are adversarial rather than collaborative. The overarching mind-set of teachers as exclusive professionals and parents as "just the parents" needs to change. School meetings can be intimidating for many parents while many have difficulty accepting the behavioral problems of their child, becoming angry, and lashing out at teachers. Also, parents more apt to attend school events and teacher conferences during their child's early elementary years, are often unavailable physically and emotionally during later school years, when many children need their support the most.

High-tech bullying is inescapable resulting in students with fragile self-esteem, anxiety, and depression. Youth who are questioning their gender identity and those with disabilities are extremely vulnerable. Even high-status youth report feeling vulnerable to forms of cyberbullying. Parental involvement is crucial because research indicates a considerable proportion of peer victimization occurs outside of school (Turner et al. 2011). Parents vigilant at home for both cyberbullying and traditional bullying can have a significant impact on the reduction of bullying often occurring outside of school and then negatively impacting the educational process in school. While we have made significant national gains in education we have not even come close to dealing with parents; we are educating for a different time and our efforts need to be redoubled (Lavoie 2010).

Research indicates conflict between children and their parents has been associated with increased bully perpetration suggesting the importance of parent-training programs. Ttofi, Farrington and Losel (2014) systematically reviewed international studies identifying the most important factors providing resilience from school bullying perpetration and bullying-victimization to maladjustment problems (internalizing and externalizing behaviors) later in life. Factors interrupting the cycle included having good performance at school and good social skills, coming from a *stable family*, being attached to *parents* and having pro-social friends. Baldry and Farrington (2005) also found supportive parenting to have a moderating effect on bullying, while students themselves reported supportive parents to be the most effective way to cope (Paul, Smith and Blumberg 2012).

Parent-child communication, meeting children's friends, and encouraging children academically were associated with lower bullying odds, suggesting protective factors of parenting needs to be considered in designing preventative interventions (Shetgiri et al. 2013). Accordino and Accordino (2011) studying cyberbullying in 6th grade students found those who had close relationships with parents were bullied less often. Students who had distant relationships with parents had higher incidences of bullying and cyberbullying. Strong parenting has also been recognized as crucial when a child has early-onset CD and ADHD. "Conduct problems are relatively stable over time and can lead to continuing difficulties in adolescence and adulthood including substance abuse, adult criminality, and relationship difficulties" (Broadhead et al. 2009, 167). Findings suggest schools and pediatricians routinely inquire about parent-child relationships and provide parent-training programs to support warmth and involvement in the family unit.

Research also indicates parents have significant stress when they have a child with challenging behaviors (Hassall et al. 2005). Parents who received increased amounts of social support in this study, who had more internal locus' of control in managing their child's behavior were found to have less parental stress. Empowering parents with the notion that they can and should manage their child's behavior while giving them tools to do so, might effectively reduce parental stress, improve the child-parent bond, and reduce bullying and victimization at school.

RETHINKING PARENT-TEACHER CONFERENCES

The traditional model of the annual school parent-teacher conference needs to be reevaluated on its efficacy on improving student behaviors and academics. Unfortunately, this model does not work well with parents who deny their child's bullying behavior or who make themselves unavailable for meetings. Parents often demonstrate a high need for power themselves and do not regard their child's behavior as a concern (Bowers, Smith and Binney 1994). Educators need to be creative, persistent, have an, "I can do attitude," and harness themselves with supports and personnel to make meetings successful despite resistant and sometimes aggressive parents. Models from other disciplines can provide clues for improving collaboration.

CASE MANAGEMENT MODEL AND HOME VISITS

A more promising practice for use in schools, used among social work professionals is the case management approach. Using this model teachers are assigned a caseload of students over a period of several years focusing on building family relationships, providing individualized supports and increasing communication. Behavioral interventions involving the family and developing strong relationships may be a more viable option for prevention of behaviors compared to semiannual parent-teacher conferences. Trust building is more likely to occur when parents and educators are given the time.

Research indicates parent training and assistance in resolving family conflict are important factors to consider in reducing bully perpetration. Creating school and family partnerships creates a trust-building situation where established lines of communication can facilitate early solutions to aggressive bullying behaviors in young children. Home visits, customary in the fields of social work and early childhood special education, provide an important dimension toward understanding the whole child. Efficacy of this approach is seen in the early intervention process established by the IDEA. Children from birth through age two are provided with services in the home to meet their needs with goals for the family as well. This proactive model has many advantages including increased communication and support to families resulting frequently in the child making increasing social, emotional, physical, and academic gains. By forging a family-school bond, benefits may include reduction in bullying, and years of trust and respect between teachers and parents. Unfortunately, schools often respond to bullying after the fact, resulting in difficult and unresolvable situations involving administrators, social workers, psychologists, teachers, and attorneys. Research findings consistently demonstrate the strength of the parent-child relationship and its direct relationship to bullying in school. Children who have conflicts with parents, or are victims of violence or neglect in the home, fair worse than peers who have good relationships with their parents. Teachers need time and compensation to meet with parents in their homes. Research on this unpracticed activity needs to be further explored.

CLINICAL TRIALS IN THE CLASSROOM

Clinical trials in medicine are used to determine the efficacy of treatment and medications. Schools need to become more research based where educational researchers conduct studies having experimental and control groups of students. Common use of meta-analyses and indirect reporting of student behavior through parental or teacher surveys have significant limitations. Unfortunately, superintendents have concerns about student privacy and concerns exist with the practice of withholding interventions from students who need them. Greater emphasis on prevention and interventions for the expected 5% of the student population that will be resistant to behavioral change is needed. The concept of teacher researcher needs to be developed and compensated for. Empirical research needs to be conducted on the efficacy of individual behavioral interventions and components of anti-bullying initiatives.

Teachers' job responsibilities need to include provisions for conducting research, and the research available should be used to drive school decisions. Professional development programs, often selected in response to the latest state education initiative, should include results from empirical studies. Professional development schools are a recent trend in education, where partnerships developed between school districts and universities model the clinical model used in medicine. Developing partnerships with universities is a win-win situation, where universities are provided with opportunities for clinical research, and districts are provided with evidence to support their programs. It is clear a new paradigm of conducting empirical research in schools is needed.

HIGHER EDUCATION TRAINING

Examining the perceptions of preservice secondary science teachers, Raven and Jurkiewicz (2014) suggest teachers felt they were not prepared to deal with bullying. Teacher certification and training programs in special education commonly include coursework dealing with characteristics of children with emotional and behavioral disorders including CD, ODD, and ADHD but this training is limited for general education teacher candidates. Furthermore, preservice and practicing teachers need extensive annual training and professional development on common psychiatric disorders in children and principles of behavior. Changing behaviors of children who bully is no easy task for even the most skilled teachers.

OBSERVATION AND RESPONSE-TO-INTERVENTION (RTI) APPROACHES

Schools need to use data to make academic, behavioral, and programmatic decisions, while teachers need training on collecting it. Teachers and support staff also need practice in observation spending periods of time observing students in structured and unstructured settings such as recess, hallways, and lunchrooms. Many schools are using RtI to screen, evaluate, deliver services and monitor the effectively academically and behaviorally. RtI, a multitiered level of support, consists of multiple layers of either academic or behavioral prevention and intervention that systematically increase in intensity. Tiers One and Two offer support for whole-school and small-group support respectively. Students who do not benefit are provided with a more intensive and individualized Tier Three intervention. It can be expected that 3–5% of the school population will need high intensity intervention.

RtI initially was used as a procedure to replace the severe discrepancy model used to identify children with learning disabilities, but more recently, this model is being used to focus attention on a student's behavioral response to evidence-based instruction through data collection and progress monitoring. Teachers, administrators, and parents have responsibilities in the implementation of RtI. "RtI comes from the confluence of a long history of applied research and practice coupled with improved engineering for delivering instruction in the real world all wrapped up in the perfect storm of political and social policy imperatives demanding better outcomes for all of our children" (Tulley 2009). Using RtI consistently to screen all children for early problematic behaviors has great potential to reduce problems of school bullying. Children with mental health disorders should be screened for bullying behavior (Benedict et al. 2014).

REFERRAL TO SPECIAL EDUCATION AND USE OF FUNCTIONAL BEHAVIORAL ASSESSMENTS AND BEHAVIOR INTERVENTION PLANS

RtI is ineffective in changing behavior in some children. It is important to watch for early red flags and respond appropriately with an initial referral to special education when a child's behavior interferes with their educational progress. RtI should never be used to delay or deny an evaluation. If a private school or outside agency, such as Head Start is located within a district's jurisdiction, a district is required to evaluate a child if they suspect the child may be eligible and conduct an evaluation within 60 days or according to the state's legal guideline. Once a district receives a child-find referral, it must initiate the evaluation process under IDEA.

Unfortunately, many districts take too long to conduct special education evaluations when the current IEP or 504 Accommodation plan is ineffective. Furthermore, they do not respond in a timely way when suspecting a child has a behavioral problem that may fall under the classification of emotional disability. When children have behaviors to a marked degree over a long period of time that are having an educational impact and do not respond to behavioral interventions, they should be referred to the multidisciplinary special education team for evaluation. The child who bullies may have an emotional disability requiring an IEP, with goals and programs to address their behavioral and emotional needs.

Many bullying programs still lack pre-planned and targeted interventions for the child who bullies despite state mandates to provide these. Using behavior analytic principles including frequent analysis and monitoring and strong continuums of support for children who bully are needed. Bullying should be addressed by conducting a functional behavioral assessment, and then the development of a behavior intervention plan based on the results (Maag and Katsiyannis 2006). Used frequently in the field of special education, this process allows for an analysis of what causes the behavior, what function it serves, and then a plan to address it. Training on performing functional behavior analyses should not be limited to psychologists, special education teachers or specialists with BCBAs (Board Certified in Behavior Analysis) but provided to parents and all who work with children in schools.

WRAPAROUND SERVICES

When intensive services of Tier Three fail to change the child's behavior, services outside school may need consideration. The wraparound process involves a team-based approach with representatives from community supports who collaborate on an intervention plan, meeting the needs of the student and his family. Research clearly indicates many children who bully need to receive mental health support. Sixteen percent of U.S. children have mental health disorders and approximately 30% of those with mental health disorders were identified as bullies (Benedict et al. 2014). Some researchers think the mental health approach may be effective because indicators of pathology occur very early in children's lives much the same way a child with ADHD begins to exhibit certain symptoms early in life (Rubin 2002). Some districts have mental health clinics on schools grounds run by nonprofit organizations that set up services to address problems in children ranging from anxiety, PTSD, depression and learning disabilities to early stages of bipolar disorder and psychosis. Treating young students may prevent the occurrence of more serious mental health disorders in later grades. Clinics in schools are also beneficial to parents and students concerned about visiting clinics in the community due to the stigma of mental health services.

TRAINING FOR BYSTANDERS

Research on the role of bystanders or defenders of victims has been studied extensively. Cowie (2014) suggests because bullying is recognized as a group process, and students themselves know the intricacies of the bully dynamic and the players, it makes sense to develop peer support systems where bystanders are empowered to support the victim. Studies indicate that having a defending behavior has the potential for achieving high social status among the peer group. Poyhonen, Juvonen and Salmivalli (2010) examined the role of cognitive, emotional and interpersonal factors predicting defending of bullied peers finding that a student's strong sense of self-efficacy and confidence in defending behavior and high social status within the peer group predicted defending behavior. Findings support interventions that encourage students with high status to defend victimized children against high-status bullies. A teacher shares her perceptions,

One situation in particular that I will never forget is when my friend was making fun of a girl that rode our bus. He constantly called her names and would even throw paper at her in hopes it would stick in her frizzy hair. I always stood up for her by telling him to stop but he never would. One day, I snapped and yelled at him and told him that as long as he treated her like that, he and I were no longer friends. I got up from my seat and sat with her. I'll never forget the look of gratitude in her tearful eyes as she thanked me. He eventually apologized to her (most likely just so he and I could be friends again) but the harassment stopped. I feel that along with helping bullies stop the behavior, it is crucial to reward students' positive behavior towards those that get bullied. As teachers teaching students to advocate for one another is an effective and positive way to approach bullying.

Unfortunately, many students are scared to report bullying for various reasons including fear of repercussions and possible retaliation of the child who bullies. A teacher shares her experience as a bystander during childhood:

Being a frightened bystander was once a role of mine in middle school. Fortunately, I was never a victim of bullying and I was never a bully. However, I was one of the students in the school who was friendly with some bullies. I associated myself with them only because I knew that it would keep me safe from being bullied or picked on. There were quite a few times that I could remember being in the back of the crowd, or standing close by while the bullies made comments about other students and picked on them for no apparent reason at all. The victims of their bullying usually were "nerds," "geeks," or "losers." I would feel awful anytime I was around them while they were making fun of other students. I knew that I didn't belong hanging out with that crowd of kids because of how bad I felt for their victims. It took at least an entire school year for me to realize that I did not want to be friends with these people any longer. The only problem was getting away from them without them turning around and bullying me.

The push to empower bystanders and increase awareness is apparent with movements such as the "no more" campaign (www.nomore.org) created to curb domestic violence and sexual assault. Schools need to adopt this approach where students of all ages buy into "no more" bullying.

DISCLOSURE OF DIFFERENCE OR
DISABILITY: TEACHING TOLERANCE

Kindergarten teachers are frequently the first to know when a student is different from peers and stands out from the rest. Parents are often reluctant to talk to the teacher about their child's differences, and teachers are reticent about talking to their students about another child's disability.

As most educators know and Dan Coulter explains (2009), "If you're the parent of a child with a disability such as Asperger Syndrome, worried about what will happen if other students find out, here's a thought; they already know." Knowing that children with differences are vulnerable to bullying, it is logical to talk to peers about each person's strengths and differences in developmentally appropriate ways. Preschool children, already very aware of differences among themselves benefit from explanations. Children who understand are more apt to show sensitivity, kindness, and helpfulness to those who are different. The majority of children, given simple information, have the potential to be extraordinarily tolerant once they understand. A teacher shares:

> Ivan was a 10-year-old non-English speaking immigrant from Bosnia, one of 28 third graders, who enjoyed being with peers in a new school community. Ivan appeared different more to adults than peers who accepted him for his wit and grit. As a bilateral amputee resulting from a land mine explosion in his home country, he was very capable of navigating the school environment either in his wheelchair or by scooting on the floor using his arms and strong upper body. During his elementary years, his classmates did not perceive him to be disabled because of his agility, pride, and humor. On the first day of middle school, I spoke to his new class about his amputations, their care, and difficulties adjusting to his new prosthetic legs. The students were kind, respectful, and helpful. Students who might have considered bullying him would not because it would not have "been cool" and they would not gain the power and status desired because Ivan was not vulnerable and bystanders were empowered.

More research needs to done on the effects of children disclosing their disabilities and its effects on reducing bully perpetration. Children may be less apt to taunt when the majority of students will not support it and vulnerable children are empowered. Children with disabilities, with parental and administrator support, can teach their classmates about their differences through various age-appropriate modalities through art, video, writing and PowerPoint presentations.

THE "COOLNESS" FACTOR

Parents continually express wanting their child to be accepted by peers, sharing tearfully how devastating it is for their child to be excluded. Additionally, educators want their students to be respectful, kind, and tolerant of each other's differences. Students want to be validated by their peers. Educators need to figure out better ways for children to achieve acceptance by peers. How can we assist all children in achieving social status among their peer group? How can we assist bully perpetrators to achieve the social status they so strongly desire in more appropriate ways? What types of replacement behaviors can be substituted for direct and covert forms of bullying? Teachers need to identify individual strengths among all children and capitalize on them giving at risk students opportunities to assist others. Reading to students in lower grades, tutoring peers in academics or athletics or assisting teachers, may provide ways to build the social power students who bully desire. Pairing children who bully with students having physical disabilities can have very beneficial effects and is worth further study.

THE NEW WAR ON CYBERBULLYING

Research demonstrates cyberbullying is distinctly different from traditional bullying. Males and females are equally likely to cyberbully. Popular students are electronically aggressive and vulnerable to victimization. Students with early behavioral risk are predicted to engage in cyberbullying later. Research suggests cyberbullying others and being a victim leads to depression and suicidal ideation in some students. In females, the more friends engaging in cyber aggression, the more likely they will use social media to do the same. Research demonstrates teachers effective in controlling traditional bullying in the classroom, may cause cyberbullying to increase. Students who would not engage in traditional bullying may engage in cyberbullying due to the disinhibition effect where they are deterred enough in school, or have enough social awareness and regard for others, but cyberbully because they do not have to face their hurt victim. They perceive teachers will still have high regard for them because they will never be caught. Since cyberbullying frequently occurs outside of school, parents must educate themselves on new features of smartphones and computers and monitor their child's cyber behaviors much the same way good parents have always monitored their children's friends, attendance at social events, and participation outside of school. Cell phones and computers, so often used for negative social interactions should be earned privileges at home and school. The protective effects of parenting on cyberbullying are very clear. Adolescents fearing parent consequences, engage in less cyberbullying. Also, parents who develop close relationships with their children, monitor friendships, and work to reduce conflict in the household will have children engaging less in cyberbullying. Schools need to do everything possible to provide parents skills with developing warm, close relationships with their children, where consequences related to technological devices are fair and consistent.

PREVENTATIVE SUPPORTS FOR HIGHLY
VULNERABLE VICTIMS

Students with disabilities and LGBT youth are highly vulnerable to bullying therefore, preventative supports are needed in school. Alternatives to the school bus, leaving early for class, staying in for recess, changing clothes for physical education classes in the nurse's office, and checking in with the student before and after school might be appropriate. Students with delayed receptive, expressive and pragmatic language skills may need peer buddies during recess and other unstructured places such as the lunchroom. Parents need to know what to do, if bullying persists. If their child is in special education and their child is not receiving a FAPE, including not going to school, parents can request a due process hearing. If bullying reaches the level of discrimination and harassment, the Office of Civil Rights should be contacted.

Students who are introverted, shy, and lack assertiveness also are vulnerable. If a child is consistently ignored by peers educators need to assist in finding outlets where the child can develop strengths and interests. Parents and educators should exercise caution when engaging vulnerable children in team sports, where coaches are not trained in bullying. Often a quiet, awkward, vulnerable child is better off competing in individualized sports such as karate, swimming, and running. Teachers and parents need to encourage friendships for those consistently marginalized and watched for the development of anxiety, depression, and fear of going to school. Parents and teachers have to learn what to do during the early school years, so children do not lose hope in adults' abilities to keep them safe.

PROVISION OF SOCIAL SUPPORTS

Research indicates social support in a student's life may influence or be related to the occurrence of violence in schools. Students without support do not enjoy its positive benefits and cause them to lash out at others (Demaray et al. 2006). Providing parents and teachers with informational support to help them learn how to recognize signs their children may be experiencing or perpetrating violence at school, and utilizing peer support groups and training students to communicate needing support for violent behavior in school may be beneficial. Benefits of close relationships with students cannot be stressed enough.

Conclusion

What the Evidence Suggests

Bullying research consistently demonstrates evidence of poor outcomes for children who bully with long-lasting consequences with later offending and criminal behavior (Ttofi and Farrington 2011). Although progress has been made in schools, bullying remains a significant and ongoing concern for teachers and administrators in the field. Research is mixed on the effectiveness of existing anti-bullying programs with evidence of schools providing programs lacking intensity, longevity, or efficacy. Sobering as the research is, acknowledging the evidence is important in planning interventions for students involved in bullying. Teachers, parents, mental health clinicians, and medical professionals need to communicate frequently when young children exhibit characteristics of bullying, because children who bully and children who are victims are vulnerable to psychiatric disorders and poor outcomes in adulthood. Educators need to understand the motivations behind bullying behaviors and be vigilant about consistently providing appropriate interventions. Simply put, children who persistently and chronically bully and their victims need help.

Schools need to go beyond generic anti-bullying interventions and identify risk profiles for children who are at greatest risk for bullying (Shetgiri 2012). They need to understand the mechanisms behind bully perpetration, considering the lasting effects on students who bully and students who are victims. "Providing psychological support to not only the victims of bullying but bullies as well cannot be overemphasized. Understanding the risk profile of childhood bullies is essential in gaining a better understanding of this public health problem and in creating useful and appropriate resources and interventions" (Benedict et al. 2014, 11). Examining predictors and supplementing the socialization approaches of anti-bullying problems with frequent systematic and long-term behavioral supports for children who bully may be beneficial. Teachers need to understand certain risk factors exist that indicate a child might bully such as being male, having aggressive parents, having ADHD, and having a CD. Gender, however plays less of a role in cyberbullying, with males and females equally likely to bully.

Educators and policy-makers by improving their abilities to identify characteristics of children related to bullying behavior can tailor interventions to meet their needs. Bullying discourse needs to reframe bullying closely considering individual risk factors with the understanding that youth bully in school in order to establish their position within their school's social hierarchy. A child who bullies does so because they are making an extreme investment in a cultural system to establish their position at the top (Bansel et al. 2009, 67). Parenting practices, comorbidity with ADHD, CD, ODD, and other predictor variables need to be considered while developing interventions. Hopefully early intervention efforts will lead to behavioral change.

Theoretical frameworks and the definitional overlap of aggression and bullying terms pose challenges for the study of bullying. Should bullying be addressed as a group process within the framework of social network (Wei and Lee 2014) or should the focus be on individual risk factors and a psychopathological approach? Both frameworks have value, however fidelity and sustainability of certain aspects may be more important than anything else. Studies have identified important considerations for inclusion in bully programs. Ansary et al. (2015) discuss critical components through examination of four anti-bullying programs studied in the meta-analyses by Craig, Pepler, Murphy et al. 2010 and Ttofi and Farrington, 2011, including the Norwegian Olweus Bullying Prevention Program (Olweus and Limber, 2010), Spain's Seville Study (Ortega, Del-Ray and Mora-Mercan, 2004) the UK's DFE Sheffield Anti-Bullying Project (Eslea and Smith, 1998) and the Finnish KiVa program (Salmivalli, Poskiparta, Ahtola and Haataja, 2013. Components included, 1) Taking an ecological perspective integrating school, family and the community 2) Taking a whole-school approach 3) Promoting a positive school climate 4) Promoting social-emotional skills and skills to diffuse conflict 5) Promoting upstanding behavior 6) Providing continuous and developmental appropriate approaches from kindergarten to grade 12 7) Strong school leadership from the principal and school board 8) Evaluation of program effectiveness 9) Coordination of an anti-bullying program with other programs 10) Teacher and staff training 11) Policies and guidance on reporting and when police should be called 12) Clearly defined consequences avoiding blame without punishment and 13) Development of a core group of individuals who coordinate resources between school and community.

While anti-bullying programs have value, proactive approaches dealing with behavioral change in the individual child who bullies needs significantly more emphasis. Significant problems exist in sustaining behavioral interventions in schools despite regulations calling for behavioral interventions for students involved in bullying (Pinkelman 2015). In this qualitative study to identify the importance of enablers and barriers to the sustainability of school-wide positive behavioral interventions and supports school personnel perceived staff buy-in, school administrative support and consistency were the most common enablers. Most commonly cited barriers were staff buy-in and resources of time and money. Often teachers were overwhelmed with curriculum, initiatives, and were not committed to supporting PBIS implementation and having to do one more thing (Pinkelman 2015).

Research demonstrates that bullying behavior is more challenging to stop than educators and mental health providers perceive and children are adept at concealing their activities. Stavrinides et al. (2014) found surprising results between children's disclosure of their activities to their parents and bullying. Hypothesizing that child disclosure would lead to less bullying, findings indicated the opposite showing an actual increase in bullying. These results imply there may be a link between child disclosure of their bullying activities and deception. Upon examination results from this study correlate with research indicating the failure of children to disclose their bullying behaviors. "Adolescents who disclose bullying others will most probably continue doing this regardless of their parents' monitoring, unless something really dramatic happens to stop them" (13). Victims of bullying are also reluctant to disclose because they are afraid their parents will overact and confront the parents of the bully, feel their parents should have known, and think telling parents confirms they are weak. Some adolescents do not disclose because in addition to being bullied, they are bullying others (DeLara 2012).

Changing the behaviors of the 5% of the school population who are predicted to engage in criminal behavior (Vaughn, 2011) is challenging. Longitudinal research in school settings needs to continue to determine what, if any interventions are effective in changing the behaviors of children who bully others. Despite calls for school reform and the development of research-based practices, school themselves are resistant to change. Are students who bully destined to go from the schoolhouse to the jailhouse? Do we have illusions of schools as innocent bystanders in the development of these particular children and pass the buck to the parents? Children with ED are often sent to alternative schools where all students have behavior disorders. Is this a research-based practice demonstrating behavioral change? Schools are not just or joyful. "Every adult who works with children in schools needs to love and respect them, to wake up each day to struggle and strive toward social justice, and to find joy and pleasure in it all, or go do something else" (Laura 2014, p. 89). Development of a more transformative and resilience-focused paradigm for schools (Nicoll 2014) with support for the development of social-emotional competencies, and strong family-school connections are called for. The research is clear across all disciplines. Healthy relationships between parents and children affect their outcomes socially, emotionally, and academically. Changing how educators relate to parents may be the most significant positive effect in education today. A study on parental stress (Hassall, Rose, and McDonald 2005) indicated parental stress was positively associated with behavioral difficulties in their child, feeling they had less control over their lives (external locus of control), and less parenting satisfaction. The results indicate the importance of incorporating behavioral training interventions to assist parents in coping with stress associated with behaviors in their children. A more clinical model is needed where parents are provided with behavioral training supports that can be harnessed when responding to behaviors in their children.

The majority of parents have difficulty dealing with behaviors in their children. In some cases when children are disrespectful, and learn to get what they want, they become successful at taking the parents' power away. Grover (2015) found that "on the surface it looks like an angry child harassing a parent who's just too tired to say 'no.' Underneath, there is much more going on. You're likely to find a child who has learned how to exploit his parents' insecurities to get what he wants. And here's the worst part: the longer a parent surrenders to the temper tantrums, threats, and manipulations, the harder it is to break these bullying tendencies. As parents cede power, children grow more aggressive. Sensing a leadership void, they begin to lose respect for their parents and decide to fill the parenting role themselves; they start to parent their parents!" Educators and clinicians need to recognize the signs of parent, child power imbalance and assist parents with behavior management training. This is especially important for professionals working with young children because they can positively influence the parent-child bond while teaching appropriate skills in managing behavior during the child's formative years. Research also suggests parents do not tell their victimized child to fight back, confront the child who bullies or the parents, ignore their child's concerns, or tell them to toughen up (Offrey and Rinaldi 2014).

Although small changes are evident, significant improvements in student behavior remains to be seen. Educational initiatives are slow to take hold in a world becoming less transparent. It is the responsibility of all school faculty and staff to identify students who bully, use interventions with fidelity, collaborate among professionals, form family partnerships, and set high expectations for appropriate behavior. Research indicates students do not perceive their teachers to be effective in keeping them safe from bullying. Bullying is often a covert and subtle behavior, and less visible than face-to-face bullying. Children who bully target the vulnerable child and will bully quietly when they know they will not get caught. If they do get caught, they have the skills to manipulate adults and successfully argue in their defense, while the victim, lacking receptive, expressive, and social skills is unable to articulate the events while misinterpreting bullying for attention and friendship. This is often the case where children on the autism spectrum or with intellectual disabilities are incessantly bullied. The impact of humiliation and shame and ability to heal from the social destruction of self may be impossible for fragile children (Martocci, 2015). Teachers need to be proficient in the use of computer-based progress monitoring, and teachers should hold high expectations for a positive school climate that is proactive, positive, and consistent with decision-making. Children who bully particularly after the age of eight may be resistant to behavioral change, implying early childhood providers need strong knowledge of behavior interventions. Schools being social entities have the ability to potentially change the behaviors of children who persistently and chronically exert their power over peers. If interventions are delivered early in a child's life, pediatricians screen both children and their parents, mental health services are more readily available to families, and educators are empowered to deliver effective and appropriate interventions for children and families, bullying should subside.

Interventions need to focus on alternative socially appropriate behaviors that afford the child who bullies the power they so desperately need. Bradshaw (2015) suggests schools' use of programs to increase social-emotional learning (SEL) and reduce aggressive and disruptive behavior by using school-wide positive behavior supports (Sugai and Horner, 2006). Durlak et al. (2011) conducted a meta-analysis of studies on SEL, finding students (kindergarten through high school) who received direct teacher instruction in SEL had significantly improved social and emotional skills, attitudes, behavior, and academic performance. Policy makers and educators, in light of provisions for SEL in the new ESEA Act, need to consider the positive impact of SEL programs in standard educational practice. Within SEL and PBIS the elementary school child who bullies can be provided with leadership positions that may provide high social status without the need to harm others in the process, while positively reinforcing pro-social behaviors at school and home.

School's reactive approach to bullying needs to be supplemented with an orientation toward a more behaviorally responsive system that considers the all important desire for all children to feel valued and an accepted part of the school social hierarchy. Teachers need to be cognizant that all children want friends but some do not know how to make them. The victim, often with disabilities and having very weak social and communication skills, or who is LGBT, is marginalized, while the child who bullies having high status and good self-esteem wants to remain at the top of the pack. Capitalizing on the strengths of each child, while working in tandem with parents, enabling them to earn the respect of classmates is important.

Research needs to continue examining the predictors and correlates of bullying behavior in children in schools while anti-bullying programs need to be diligently monitored for success. A proactive interdisciplinary approach is needed where tertiary, intense supports and special education programming are used to change behaviors of children who bully. Engaging intensive supports and developing strong alliances with parents early in the child's educational career when behaviors manifest will reduce bullying's irreparable effects to the individual child, the victims, schools, communities, and society. School psychologists are unable to tackle the bullying problem alone because on the basis of the average school psychologist–to–student ratio of 1:1, 400 (Charvat, 2011), there is not enough time in the day for work with students, teachers and parents. The needs of students and their parents can be serious and intense; students with emotional disabilities are found to be at the greatest risk of being bullied and need preventative care and supports along with their parents (Bear et al. 2015).

Cyberbullying poses large challenges for school and families because a substantial number of incidents occur outside school hours, many events are anonymous, and there are immediate effects on potentially large number of students. In a recent study, Carter (2015) found most adolescents have access to cell phones (80%) and computers (80–90%) with males and females equally likely to cyberbully primarily using social networking sites. Adolescent use of the Internet has become an accepted behavior and schools and parents are not aware of the implications including dangers and associated psychosocial issues later in adulthood. The covert nature of cyberbullying, and reluctance of children who disclose bullying or victimization poses a great challenge for parents and teachers. Educators and school administrators also have great concern with the secondary negative effects of bullying and its disruption to the learning process.

Studies worldwide have considered the influence of genetic and environmental factors on behavior. Chen et al. (2015) studying 908 Chinese pairs of adolescent twins found aggressive behavior to be influenced moderately by genetic factors. Although associations between the individual's biological and aggressive behaviors were found, this study also suggests that cultural values attenuate genetic potential in externalizing behaviors such as aggression. Most of us have difficulty accepting the scientific fact that a newborn may already have a genetic predisposition to aggression or bullying. Although more research needs to be conducted this troubling finding indicates a strong need of early environment influences to counteract these behaviors.

Educator's prevailing notion of bullies as having poor self-esteem and lack of awareness of childhood psychiatric disabilities indicate a strong need for training among pre-service and in-service teachers and support staff. The ineffective practices of suspension and expulsion need to be replaced with planned practices that effectively change behavior, that ultimately are endorsed by school boards and their attorneys. Stronger articulation agreements between schools and law enforcement need to be forged, with an end to practices stigmatizing schools for reporting violent incidences. Schools need mechanisms to support professional development and provide intense training in behavioral intervention and support. Providing more than the customary handful of professional development days annually can serve to increase educator buy-in for PBIS programs, cited as a barrier to its use. Para-educators and all school support staff need education and a clear definition of job responsibilities in recognizing and reporting bullying. Training also needs to include teachers of preschool students. Manifestation of aggressive behaviors in early childhood indicates a need for parents and teachers to intervene early. School shootings, although rare compared to the daily and common occurrence of bullying, necessitates a stronger system of behavioral prevention and safety in schools. Schools need to understand and adopt threat assessment approaches and routinely assign and train teachers for crisis teams preparing for problematic events.

States' adoption of anti-bullying laws will have a positive effect on increasing educator awareness and reporting bullying, but federal and state laws reportedly overlap and are confusing (Zirkel, 2014). School leaders need to diligently train teachers in discrimination, harassment, and bullying laws and their implications, consulting school attorneys when difficult cases arise. Proactively communicating with community law enforcement can provide channels for problem-solving especially with the rise of cyberbullying and bullying off school grounds. Parents and schools need to keep abreast of new technology including apps, social media, and GPS that can potentially harm and aggressively monitor student use of digital devices. Schools should dedicate a staff member to research new technology and provide workshops for parents and educators.

Special education procedures need to be followed per state and federal law. Schools have a legal obligation to find and evaluate children suspected of having a disability that interferes with accessing the school curriculum. Schools often wait to refer children with aggressive behaviors and use the RtI process to delay referral. Schools are under pressure to keep their special education numbers down given the expense of services and multidisciplinary teams and are reluctant to suggest psychiatric evaluations for the same reasons.

All children are potential victims, particularly if they are different, however educators should realize those with disabilities and those who are LGBT are extremely vulnerable without supports. Children who bully seek out those most vulnerable and fragile. Although suicide is a relatively uncommon event and studies challenge simple cause-and-effect models that may suggest that suicide arises from any one factor, such as bullying (Sinyor 2014), educators need to understand warning signs and relationships between bullying and suicide. Suicide in youth is recognized as a complex interplay of various biological, psychological, and social factors of which bullying is only one. Reviewing coroner records for all suicide deaths in Toronto youth bullying was present in six deaths (6.4%) whereas any stressor or mental and or physical illness was detected in 78.7% of cases. The most common stressors identified were conflict with parents (21.3%), romantic partner problems (17.0%), academic problems (10.6%), and criminal and (or) legal problems (10.6%). Depression was detected in 40.4% of cases.

Victimization and bullying continue to lack intensity of counseling despite state mandates to develop policies to direct staff to provide support and referrals for students who engage in bullying (Kowalski, Limber and Agatston 2012). Parent involvement consistently identified by research as an essential component in anti-bullying programs is minimal (Gross, Breitenstein, Eisbach, Hope and Harrison 2014). SBMH models do not exist and community-based prevention activities are rare (Holt, Raczynskib, Frey, Hymel and Limber 2013). Although there is some support for the effectiveness of school-based bullying interventions overall reductions in bullying have not yet been realized. Research suggests the need to more effectively integrate school-based efforts with community-based efforts and integrate home-school bullying prevention and the role of parents in response (Lovegrove, Bellmore, Greif Green, Jens, and Ostrov 2013). "Understanding the impact of peer victimization from a mental health perspective is especially significant for mental health practitioners, researchers, and those in the healthcare field. The relevant data can be employed to develop effective early prevention and intervention programs. In order to build alliances that encourage effective solutions to be improved upon and implemented, researchers will have to form strong relationships with clinicians, speech-language pathologists, healthcare professionals, and community organizations that deal specifically with this pervasive, troubling, and highly influential issue. Directing the necessary attention, ongoing research, and allocation of appropriate resources, will further aid in the psychological relief effort that every child, both the victim and their bully, so desperately requires" (Edery et al. 2015, 582).

July 2015 marks the 25th anniversary of the Americans with Disabilities Act, one of the most important civil right laws in history. President George H. W. Bush signed this legislation to address the discrimination and physical and mental barriers faced by individuals with disabilities in school, in the community, on the job, in transportation, telecommunications and more (ADA.gov). The confluence of the reauthorization of the ESEA, the anniversary of both the IDEA and ADA, mark an important time for equality and rights of individuals in the United States. This is an opportune time to renew efforts to provide mental health services for all children who need them and to address the persistence of bullying in school. It is time for all individuals to work in harmony in order to consider what the evidence suggests in planning the best programs and procedures for ensuring schools and communities are places focusing on tolerance, safety, equal opportunity, and learning. Society should be more appalled and disappointed with the lack of legislation protecting our children in schools. Although anti-bullying laws may be a start, schools cannot serve children who bully and children who are victims alone. It is unthinkable that children, the most vulnerable population of our society have the least legal protection from harm. The mind-set needs to change where children have protections in schools, and educators and administrators can easily report bullying and victimization without legal repercussions. Significant work remains to be done by schools, communities, mental health providers, and law enforcement before we can expect bullying to decrease. Our children are still in danger as they begin their day riding the school bus because schools and communities have not been aggressive enough in reducing bullying in significant ways.

A proactive approach involves continued interdisciplinary study of psychiatric and criminology research while bullying curricula continues to be developed. These important insights will offer guidance as appropriate staff training and interventions are developed for children at risk for bullying perpetration. One thing is clear. Research indicates without intervention, children exhibiting bullying behaviors will have poor outcomes into adulthood. Educators who understand are in a better position to promote earlier and appropriate intervention for children who chronically and persistently engage in bullying behaviors. Districts need to develop protocols for the provision of counseling and behavioral intervention and be diligent and persistent in efforts in dealing with students who bully and their families.

One female, now a teacher, recalls her childhood:

I can remember being afraid to ride the bus because I knew that my brother and I were the likely targets for bullying. I was shy and less likely to stand up for myself, and my brother had different interests than other students and this made him a social outcast. I don't remember if I tried to stand up for my brother who was the main target of bullying on the bus but I think at the time I didn't have the inner strength to do so. I also distinctly remember having my seat next to a bully in elementary school. I was the type of student who cried everyday in school because I wanted to go home and I think children took advantage of this. I don't think my teachers knew exactly how to handle this because I only remember having my seat moved. As a young adult I can reluctantly state that a former boyfriend has harassed me for months, which honestly looked a lot like cyberbullying. This is why I think bullying looks different at different ages but still has the same intent in person, on the Internet or on the phone. In elementary school the bullies took advantage of a seemingly weak student, and even in college it continued with different people. It is scary to me that at twenty-two years old I can say that I have been bullied within the past six months.

No student should be afraid . . . no parent should need to worry about such things happening to their child (Olweus 1993). Unfortunately, many students are still very afraid to go to school, children's bullying behaviors persist from year to year, and families desperate to end victimization resort to transferring their child elsewhere. Bullying is often a subtle and covert activity, missed by parents and teachers. Examining the research evidence, sharing findings with practitioners and increasing communication with all those involved are important. If bullying can be curtailed, implications are broad for the well-being of all children, schools, families, and communities. As a nation, we also need to respond to the bullying problem by improving communication between pediatric mental health providers, pediatricians, parents, and educators. The integration of remediation and intervention efforts, and improved communication might assist with reducing school tragedies that persistently occur.

Bibliography

Accordino, D. B., and Accordino, M. P. 2011. An exploratory study of face-to-face and cyber bullying in sixth grade students. *American Secondary Education* 41: 14–30.

Allen, K. P. 2014. Tweeting, texting, and Facebook postings: Stirring the pot with social media to make drama – case study and participant Observation. *The Qualitative Report* 19 (2) (January 13): 1–24.

Al-Zahrani, A. M. 2015. Cyberbullying among Saudi's higher-education students: Implications for educators and policymakers. *World Journal of Education* 5 (3): 15. doi:http://dx.doi.org/10.5430/wje.v5n3p15. http://0-search.proquest.com. library.dowling.edu/docview/1691073004?accountid=10549

American Psychiatric Association. 2013. Diagnostic and statistical manual of mental disorders: 5th ed. Washington, DC: American Psychiatric Association. www.dsm5.org

American Psychiatric Association. 2000. Diagnostic and statistical manual of mental disorders: 4th ed. Washington, DC: American Psychiatric Association.

American Academy of Pediatrics 2011. *State government affairs: State legislation report 2010.* http://www.aap.org/advocacy/statelegrpt.pdf.

Ansary, N. S., Elias, M. J., Greene, M., and Green, S. 2015. Guide for schools selecting anti-bullying approaches. Translating evidence-based strategies to contemporary implementation realities. *Educational Researcher* 44 (1): 27–36.

Aronson, E. 2000. *Nobody left to hate: Teaching compassion after Columbine.* W.H. Freeman and Co: New York.

Asperger, H. 1944. Autistic psychopathology in childhood. Translated by Uta Frith. In U. Frith (ed.). *Autism & Asperger syndrome* (pp. 37–92). Cambridge, England: Cambridge University Press.

Astor, R. A., Cornell, D. G., Espelage, D. L., Furlong, M. J., Jimerson, S. R., Mayer, M. J., Nickerson, A. B., Osher, D., and Sugai, G. 2013. A call for more effective prevention of violence. *The School Psychologist* 67: 40–43.

Ayernibiowo, K. O. 2011. Psychopathology of bullying and emotional abuse among school children. *Ife Psychologia* 19: 127–141.

Badaly, D., Kelly, B. M., Schwartz, D., and Dabney-Lieras, K. 2013. Longitudinal associations of electronic aggression and victimization with social standing during adolescence. *Journal of Youth and Adolescence* 42 (6): 891–904.

Badash, D. 2015. Breaking News: Republican U.S. senators kill LGBT students' antibullying bill. www.thenewcivilrights movement.com.

Baldry, A. C. 2003. Bullying in schools and exposure to domestic violence. *Child Abuse and Neglect* 27: 713–773.

Baldry, A. C., and Farrington, D. P. 2005. Protective factors as moderators of risk factors in adolescence bullying. *Social Psychology of Education* 8: 264–284.

Bansel, P., Davies, B., Laws, C., and Linnell, S. 2009. Bullies, bullying and power in the contexts of schooling. *British Journal of Sociology or Education* 30: 59–69.

Baron-Cohen, S. 2000. Is Asperger syndrome/high functioning autism necessarily a disability? *Development and Psychopathology* 12: 489–500.

Barrett, S., Eber, L., and Weist, M. (Eds). 2013. Advancing education effectiveness: Interconnecting school mental health and school-wide positive behavior support. NASDSE, Alexandra, VA. http://www.pbis.org/common/pbisresources/publications/Final-Monograph.pdf.

Barry, C. T., Frick, P. J., DeShazo, T. M., McCoy, M. G., Ellis M., and Loney, B. R. 2000. The importance of callous-unemotional traits for extending the concept of psychopathy to children. *Journal of Abnormal Psychology* 109: 335–340.

Bear, G., Mantz, L. Glutting, J., and Yang, C. 2015. Differences in Bullying Victimization Between Students with and without Disabilities. *School Psychology Review*, 2015, 44 (1): 98–116.

Benedict, F. T., Vivier, P. M., and Gjelsvik, A. 2014. Mental health and bullying in the United States among children aged to 17 years. *Journal of Interpersonal Violence* 1–14. doi:10.1177/0886260514536279.

Besag, V. E. 2006. Bullying among girls: Friends or foes. *School Psychology International* 27: 535–551.

Björkqvist, K., and Österman, K. 2014. Does childhood physical punishment predispose to a "victim personality"? *Pediat Therapeut* 4: 190. doi:10.4172/2161-0665.1000190.

Blake, J. J., Kim, E. S., and Lease, A. M. 2011. Exploring the incremental validity of nonverbal social aggression: The utility of peer nominations. *Merrill – Palmer Quarterly* 57: 293–318.

Blake, J. J., Lund, E. M., Zhoi, Q., Kwok, O., and Benz, M. R. 2012. National prevalence rates of bully victimization among students with disabilities in the United States. *School Psychology Quarterly* 27: 210–222.

Board of Education Hendrick Hudson School District v. Rowley, 458 U.S. 176, 1982.

Book, A., Volk, A. A., and Hosker, A. 2012. Adolescent Bullying and Personality: An Adaptive Approach. *Personality and Individual Differences* 52: 218–223. doi:10.1016/j.paid.2011.10.028.

Bonanno, R. A., and Hymel, S. 2013. Cyber bullying and internalizing difficulties: Above and beyond the impact of traditional forms of bullying. *Journal of Youth and Adolescence* 42: 685–697.

Boulton, M. J., and Smith, P. K. 1994. Bully/victim problems in middle-school children: Stability, self-perceived competence, peer perceptions and peer acceptance. *British Journal of Developmental Psychology* 12: 315–329.

Bowers, L., Smith, P. K., and Binney, V. 1994. Perceived family relationships of bullies, victims, and bully/victims in middle childhood. *Journal of Social and Personal Relationships* 11: 215–232.

Bowker, J. C., Adams, R. E., Fredstrom, B. K., and Gilman, R. 2014. Experiences of being ignored by peers during late adolescence: Linkages to psychological maladjustment. *Merrill – Palmer Quarterly* 60: 328–354.

Bradshaw, C. P. 2015. Translating research to practice in bullying prevention. *American Psychologist* 70: 322–332.

Bradshaw, C. A., Sawyer, A., and O'Brennan, L. 2007. Bullying and peer victimization at school: Perceptual differences between students and school staff. *School Psychology Review* 36: 361–382.

Bradshaw, C. P., Waasdorp, T., Goldweber, A., and Johnson, S. L. 2013. Bullies, gangs, drugs, and school: Understanding the overlap and the role of ethnicity and urbanicity. Special Issue: Correlates and Consequences of Antisocial Behavior among Low Income, Urban Youth. *Journal of Youth and Adolescence* 42: 220–234.

Bradshaw, C., Waasdorp, T. E., O'Brennan, L. M., and Gulematova, M. 2013. Teachers and educator support professionals' perspectives on bullying and previous findings from a National Educational Association Study. *School Psychology Review* 42: 280–297.

Broadhead, M., Hockaday, A., Zahra, M., Francis, P., and Crichton, C. 2009. Scallywags—an evaluation of a service targeting conduct disorders at school and at home. *Educational Psychology in Practice* 25: 167–179.

Byrne, B. J. 1994. Bully and victims in school setting with reference to some Dublin schools. *Irish Journal of Psychology* 15: 574–586.

California Safe Schools Coalition & 4-H Center for Youth Development, University of California, Davis. 2004. *Consequences of harassment based on actual or Perceived sexual orientation and gender non-conformity and steps to making schools safer.* San Francisco and Davis, CA: Authors.

Camera, L. 2015, July 18. Senate passes ESEA rewrite with big bipartisan backing 81–17. *Education Week.*

Camodeca, M., and Goossens, F. A. 2005. Aggression, social cognitions, anger and sadness in bullies and victims. *Journal of Child Psychology and Psychiatry* 46: 186–197.

Cappadocia, M. C., Weiss, J. A., and Pepler, D. 2011. Bullying experiences among children and youth with autism spectrum disorders. *Journal of Autism and Development Disorders* 42: 266–277. doi 10.1007/s10803-011-1241-x.

Card, N. 2011. Toward a relationship perspective on aggression among schoolchildren: Integrating social cognitive and interdependence theories. *Psychology of Violence* 1 (3): 188–201.

Cardoos, S. L., and Hinshaw, S. P. 2011. Friendship as protection from peer victimization for girls with and without ADHD. *Journal of Abnormal Child Psychology* 39 (7) (10): 1035–1045.

Carter, J. M., and Feleta L. W. 2015. Cyberbullying: A 21st century health care phenomenon. *Pediatric Nursing* 41 (3): 115–125. http://0-search.proquest.com.library. dowling.edu/docview/1687982550?accountid=10549.

Carter, S. 2009. Bullying of students with Asperger syndrome. *Issues in Comprehensive Pediatric Nursing* 32 (3): 145–154.

Carter, S. 2005. Comparison of children and adolescents with Asperger syndrome to their peers with learning disabilities in adaptive functioning, academic achievement,and victimization. *Dissertation Abstracts International* 66 (01) UMI. No. 3160618.

Casebeer, C. M. 2012. School bullying: Why quick fixes do not prevent school failure. *Preventing School Failure* 54: 165–171.

Chen, P., and Schwartz, I. S. 2012. Bullying and victimization experiences of students with autism spectrum disorders in elementary schools. *Focus on Autism and Other Developmental Disabilities* 27 (4): 200–212.

Chen, J., Yu, J., Zhang, J., Li, X., and McGue, M. 2015. Investigating genetic and environmental contributions to adolescent externalizing behavior in a collectivistic culture: a multi-informant twin study. *Psychological Medicine* 45 (9): 1989–1997. doi:http://dx.doi.org/10.1017/S0033291714003109.

Cho, J., Hendrickson, J. M., and Mock, D. R. 2009. Bullying status and behavior patterns of preadolescents and adolescents with behavioral disorders. *Education and Treatment of Children* 32: 655–671.

Claire, F. G., Poskiparta, E., and Salmivalli, C. 2014. Tackling acute cases of school bullying in the KiVa anti-bullying program: A comparison of two approaches. *Journal of Abnormal Child Psychology* 42 (6), 981–991. doi:http://dx.doi.org/10.1007/s10802-014-9861-1.

Coker, T. R., Austin, S. B., and Schuster, M. A. 2010. The health and health care of lesbian, gay, and bisexual adolescents. *Annual Review of Public Health* 31: 457–477.

Cole, C. M., Cornell, D. G., and Sheras, P. 2006. Identification of school bullies by survey methods. *Professional School Counseling* 9: 305–314.

Coloroso, B. 2003. *The bully, the bullied and the bystander.* New York: Harper-Collins Publishers. Conduct Problems Prevention Research Group. 2004. The effects of the fast track program on serious problem outcomes at the end of elementary school. *Journal of Clinical Child and Adolescent Psychology* 33 (4): 650–651. doi: 10.1207/s15374424jccp3304_1.

Cornell, D., and Limber, S. 2015. Law and policy in the concept of bullying at school. *American Psychologist* 333–343.

Cook, C. R., Williams, K. R., Guerra, N. G., Kim, T. E., and Sadek, S. 2010. Predictors of victimization in childhood and adolescence: A meta-analytic investigation. *School Psychology Quarterly* 25: 65–83.

Coolidge, F. L., DenBoer, J. W., and Segal, D. L. 2004. Personality and neuropsychological correlates of bullying behavior. *Personality and Individual Differences* 36: 1559–1569.

Cooper, L. A., and Nickerson, A. B. 2013. Parent retrospective recollections of bullying and current views, concerns, and strategies to cope with children's bullying. *Journal of Child and Family Studies* 22: 526–540.

Copeland, W. E., Wolke, D., Angold, A. E., and Costello, J. 2013. Adult psychiatric outcomes of bullying and being bullied by peers in childhood and adolescence *JAMA Psychiatry* 70: 419–426. doi:10.1001/jamapsychiatry.2013.504.

Copeland, W. E., Wolke, D., Lereya, S. T., Shanahan, L., Worthman, C., and Costello, E. J. 2014. Childhood bullying involvement predicts low-grade systemic inflammation into adulthood. *Proceedings of the National Academy of Sciences,* 111 (21): 7570–7575.

Coulter, D. 2009. They Know: Classmates and Asperger syndrome: Retrieved from www.coultervideo.com/articles.htm

Cowie, H. 2014. Understanding the role of bystanders and peer support in school bullying. *International Journal of Emotional Education* 6 (1) (04): 26–32.

Craig, K., Bell, B., and Leschied, A. 2011. Pre-service teachers' knowledge and attitudes regarding school-based bullying. *Canadian Journal of Education* 34 (2): 21–33.

Craig, W., Herel-Fish, Y., Fogel-Grinvald, H., Dostaler, S., Hetland, J., Simons-Morton, B., and Pickett, W. 2009. A cross-national profile of bullying and victimization among adolescents in 40 countries. *International Journal of Public Health* 54: 216–224.

Craig, W., Pepler, D., and Blais, J. 2007. Responding to bullying. *School Psychology International* 28: 465.

Crick, N. R., and Grotpeter, J. K. (1995). Relational aggression, gender, and social-psychological adjustment. *Child Development* 66 (3): 710–722.

Crothers, L. M., and Kolbert, J. B. 2008. Tackling a problematic behavior management issue: Teachers' intervention in childhood bullying problems. *Intervention in School and Clinic* 43: 132–139.

Cuervo, A., Martínez, E., Quintana, J., and Amezaga, T. 2014. Differences in types and technological means by which Mexican high schools students perform cyber bullying: Its relationship with traditional bullying. *Journal of Educational and Developmental Psychology* 4 (1) (05): 105–113.

Cunningham, P. B., Henggeler, S.W., Limber, S. P., Melton, G. B., and Nation, M. A. 2000. Patterns and correlates of gun ownership among nonmetropolitan and rural middle school students. *Journal of Clinical Child Psychology* 29: 432–442.

Davis v. Monroe Country Board of Education, 1999 119 S. Ct. 1661

DeLara, E. 2010. Why adolescents don't discuss incidents of bullying and harassment. *Journal of School Violence* 11, 288–305.

Demaray, M.K., Malecki, C.K., and DeLong, L.K. 2006. Support in the lives of aggressive students, their victims, and their peers (pp. 21–29). In S. R. Jimerson and M. J. Furlong (Eds.). *Handbook of School Violence and School Safety: From Research to Practice.* Mahwah, NJ: Lawrence Erlbaum Associates, Inc.

Dijkstra, J. K., Lindenberg, S., and Veenstra R. 2008. Beyond the class norm: Bullying behavior of popular adolescents and its relation to peer acceptance and rejection. *Journal of Abnormal Child Psychology* 36: 1289–1299.

DiLalla, L. F., and Gheyara, J. S. 2014. Genetic and behavioral influences on received aggression during observed play among unfamiliar preschool-aged peers. *Merrill–Palmer Quarterly* 60: 168–192.

Duchnowski, A. J., Kutash, K., Green, A. L., Ferron, J. M., Wagner, M., and Vengrofski, B. 2012. Parent support services for families of children with emotional disturbances served in elementary school special education settings: Examination of data from the special education elementary longitudinal study. *Journal of Disability Policy Studies* 24 (1): 36.

Durlak, J. A., Dymnicki, A. B. Taylor, R. D., Weissberg, R. P., and Schellinger, K.B. 2011. The impact of enhancing students' social and emotional learning: A meta-analysis of school-based universal interventions. *Child Development* 82 (1): 405–432.

Duncan, R. D. 2004. The impact of family relationships on school bullies and victims. In D. L. Espelage, & S. M. Swearer (Eds.) *Bullying in American schools: A social-ecological perspective on prevention and intervention* (pp. 227–244). Mahwah, NJ: Lawrence Erlbaum.

Eber, L., Weist, M., and Barrett, S. 2013. In *Advancing educational effectiveness: Interconnecting school mental health and school-wide positive behavior supports.* Barrett, S., Eber, L., and Weist, M. Eds. *Center for School Mental Health.*

Edery, R. 2015. Childhood peer victimization as a predictor of adolescent loneliness – A critical review of the literature. *International Journal of Emergency Mental Health and Human Resilience* 17: 581–582.

Elledge, L. C., Williford, A., Boulton, A. J., Depaolis, K. J., Little, T. D., and Salmivalli, C. 2013. Individual and contextual predictors of cyber bullying: The influence of children's provictim attitudes and teachers' ability to intervene. *Journal of Youth and Adolescence* 42 (5): 698–710.

Elsaesser, C., Gorman-Smith, D., and Henry, D. 2013. The role of the school environment in relational aggression and victimization. *Journal of Youth and Adolescence* 42 (2): 235–249. doi:http://dx.doi.org/10.1007/s10964-012-9839-7.

Emond, A., Ormel, J., Veenstra, R., and Oldehinkel, A. 2007. Preschool behavioral and social-cognitive problems as predictors of (pre)adolescent disruptive behavior. *Child Psychiatry and Human Development.* Equal Protection Clause of the Fourteenth Amendment, U.S. Constitution, Amend. XIV.

Espelage, D., Anderman, E., Brown V., Jones, A., Lane, K., McMahon, S., Reddy, L., and Reynold, C., 2013. Understanding and preventing violence directed against teachers: Recommendations for a National research, practice, and policy agenda. *American Psychologist* 68 (2): 75–87.

Espelage, D., Low, S., Rao, M., Hong, J., Little, T. 2013. Family violence, bullying, fighting, and substance use among adolescents: A longitudinal meditational model. *Journal of Research on Adolescence* 1–13. doi: 10/1111/jora.12060

Espelage, D. L., and Swearer, S. M. ed. 2004. *Bullying in American Schools: A Social-Ecological Perspective on Prevention and Intervention.* Lawrence Erlbaum Associates: New Jersey.

Fabiano, G. A., Pelham, W. E., Coles, E. K., Gnagy, E. M., Chronis-Tuscano, A., and O'Connor, B.C. 2009. A meta-analysis of behavioral treatments for attention-deficit/hyperactivity disorder. *Clinical Psychology Review* 29: 129–140.

Fallon, H. (2010, January) Building Communication Between Educators and Families is the Key to Success! Gurneys Inn, Montauk, NY.

Faris, R., and Felmlee, D. 2011. Status struggles: Network centrality and gender segregation in same- and cross-gender aggression. *American Sociological Review* 76: 48–73.

Farrington, D. P., and Baldry, A. C. 2010. Individual risk factors for school bullying. *Journal of Aggression, Conflict and Psychology Research* 2 (1): 4-16.

Farrington, D. P., and Ttofi. M. M., 2011. Bullying as a predictor of offending, violence and later life outcomes. *Criminal Behaviour and Mental Health* 21: 90–98.

Farrington, D. P., and Ttofi, M. M. 2009. School-based programs to reduce bullying and victimization (Campbell systematic reviews No. 6) Oslo, Norway: Campbell Corporation. http://dx.doi.org/10.4073/csr2009.6.

Fein, R., Vosselkuil, B., Pollack, W., Borum, R., Modzeleski, W., and Reddy, M. 2004. *Threat assessment in schools: A guide to managing threatening situations and to creating safe school climates.* United States Secret Service and United States Department of Education, Washington, D.C.

Fekkes, M., Pijpers, F. I., Fredriks, A. M., Vogels, T., and Verloove-Vanhorick, S. P. 2006. Do bullied children get ill, or do ill children get bullied? A prospective cohort study on the relationship between bullying and health-related symptoms. *Pediatrics* 117: 1568–1574.

Ferrans, S. D., and Silman, R. 2014. *Harvard Educational Review* 84: 2162–2187.

Fite, P. J., Evans, S. C., Cooley, J. L., and Rubens, S. L. 2014. Further evaluation of associations between attention-deficit/hyperactivity and oppositional defiant disorder symptoms and bullying-victimization in adolescence. *Child Psychiatry and Human Development* 45: 32–41.

Finkelhor, D., and Browne, A. 1985. The traumatic impact of child sexual abuse: A conceptualization. *American Journal of Orthopsychiatry* 55: 530–541 doi: 10.1111/j.1939-0025.1985.tb02703.x.

Forness, S. R. 2003. Barriers to evidence-based treatment: Developmental psychopathology and the interdisciplinary disconnect in school mental health practice. *School Psychology* 41: 61–67.

Frenette, L. 2014, March, p. 16–17. A push for safer schools: NYSUT presses lawmakers to include schools in the Workplace Violence Prevention Act. www.nysut.org.

Fryling, M., Cotler, J., Rivituso, J., Mathews, L., and Practico, S. 2015. Cyberbullying or Normal Game Play? Impact of age, gender, and experience on cyberbullying in multi-player online gaming environments: Perceptions from one gaming forum. *Journal of Information Systems Applied Research* 8: 1–18.

Gamm, S. January 27, 2009. Organizing a Delivery system: From law to practice. Long Island Association of Special Education Administrators Winter Conference. Public Consulting Group.

Gay, Lesbian and Straight Education Network 2009. The 2009 national school climate survey. 25–29 (2010), available at http://www.glsen.org/binary-data/GLSEN_ATTACHMENTS/file/16000/001/1675–1.pdf

Georgiou, S. N., and Stavrinides, P. 2013. Parenting at home and bullying at school. *Social Psychology of Education* 165–179.

Ghaziuddin, M. Weidmer-Mikhail, W., and Ghaziuddin, N. 1998. Comorbidity of Asperger syndrome: A preliminary report. *Journal of Intellectual Disability Research* 42: 279–283.

Gladden, R. M., Vivolo-Kantor, A. M., Hamburger, M. E., and Lumpkin, C. D. 2014. *Bullying Surveillance among Youths: Uniform Definitions for Public Health and Recommended Data Elements, Version 1.0.* Atlanta, GA; National Center for

Injury Prevention and Control, Centers for Disease Control and Prevention and U.S. Department of Education.

Goldman, C. 2012. *Bullied: What every parent, teacher and kid needs to know about ending the cycle of fear.* Harper-Collins: New York.

Goldweber, A., Waasdorp, T. E., and Bradshaw, C. P. 2013. Examining associations between race, urbanicity, and patterns of bullying involvement. *Journal of Youth and Adolescence* 42: 206–219.

Graham, S., and Juvonen, J. 1998. A social cognitive perspective on peer aggression and victimization. *Annals Child Development*, 13: 21–66.

Greene, D. C., Britton, P., and Fitts, B. 2014. Long-term outcomes of lesbian, gay, bisexual, and transgender recalled school victimization. *Journal of Counseling & Development* 92 (4): 406–417.

Greene, M. B. 2000. Bullying and harassment in schools. In R.S. Moser, & C. E. Frantz (Eds.). *Shocking violence* (pp. 72–101). Springfield, IL: Charles Thomas.

Greene, M. B. 2003. Counseling and climate change as treatment modalities for bullying in school. *International Journal for the Advancement of Counseling* 25: 293–302.

Gross, D., Breitenstein, S., Eisbach, S., Hoppe, E., and Harrison, J. 2014. Promoting Mental Health in Early Childhood Programs: Serving Low-Income Ethnic Minority Families. In M. Weist, N. Lever, C. Bradshaw, & J. Owens (Eds.), *Handbook of school mental health* (2nd ed., pp. 119–130). New York, NY: Springer. http:// dx.doi.org/10.1007/978-1-4614-7624-5_9.

Grover, S. 2005. Are you a bullied parent? *Huffington Post.* Halpern, J., and Douglas, J. 2015. Social dominance, school bullying, and child health: What are our ethical obligations to the very young? *Pediatrics* 135: S24–S30.

Hamby, S., Finkelhor, D., and Turner, H. 2013. Perpetrator and victim gender patterns for 21 forms of youth victimization in the national survey of children's exposure to violence. *Violence and Victims* 28: 915–939.

Hanish, L. D., Kochenderfer-Ladd, B., Fabes, R. A., Martin, C. L., and Dening, D. 2004. Bullying Among Young Children: The Influence of Peers and Teachers (Espelage, D. L., and Swearer, S. M. ed. 2004. *Bullying in American Schools: A Social-Ecological Perspective on Prevention and Intervention.*

Harvard Law Review (2015). Juvenile justice: In re D.S. Iowa supreme court holds that evidence of taunting is insufficient to constitute criminal harassment. 128 (7): 2058. harvardlawreview.org/2015/05/In-re-d-s/

Hassall, R., Rose, J., and McDonald, J. 2005. Parenting stress in mothers of children with an intellectual disability: The effects of parental cognitions in relation to child characteristics and family support. *Journal of Intellectual Disability Research* 49: 405–418.

Hawley, P. H., Johnson, S. E., Mize, J. A., and McNamara, K. A. 2007. Physical attractiveness in preschoolers: Relationships with power, status, aggression and social skills. *Journal of School Psychology* 45: 499–521.

Haynie, D. L., Nansel, T., Eitel, P., Crump, A. D., Saylor, L., Yu, K., and Simons-Morton, B. (2001). Bullies, victims and bully/victims: Distinct groups of at-risk youth. *Journal of Early Adolescence* 21: 29–49.

Heinrichs, R. 2003. *Perfect targets: Asperger syndrome and bullying. Practical solutions for surviving the social world.* Shawnee Mission, Kansas: Autism Asperger Publishing Company.

Hemphill, S., Kotevski, A., Tollit, M., Smith, R., Herrenkohl, T. I., Toumbourou, J. W., and Catalano, R. 2012. Longitudinal predictors of cyber and traditional bullying perpetration in Australian secondary school students. *Adolescent Health and Medicine* 51 (1): 59–65.

Henry, S. 2004. Bullying-Like father like son? The contentious findings of a yearlong study. *Education Journal* 77: 23–26.

Herman, K., Borden, L., Reinke, W., and Webster-Stratton, C. 2011. The impact of the incredible years parent, child, and teacher training programs on children's co-occurring internalizing symptoms. *School Psychology Quarterly* 26: 189–201. doi: 10.1037/a0025228

Hilton J., Anngela-Cole, L., and Wakita, J. 2010. A cross-cultural comparison of factors associated with school bullying in Japan and the United States. *Family Journal, 18*: 413.

Hinduja, S., and Patchin, J. W. 2015. Responding to cyberbullying: Top Ten Tips for Educators. Cyberbullying Research Center. www.cyberbullying.us/Top-Ten-Tips-Educators-Cyberbullying-Response.pdf

Hinduja, S., and Patchin, J.W. 2013. Social influences on cyber bullying behaviors among middle and high school students. *Journal of Youth and Adolescence* 42: 711–722.

Hinduja, S., and Patchin, J. W. 2012. State cyber bullying laws. www.cyberbullying.us/Bullying_and_Cyberbullying_Laws.pdf

Hinduja S., and Patchin, J. W. 2009. *Bullying Beyond the Schoolyard: Preventing and Responding to Cyber bullying.*

Hirsch, L., and Lower, C. 2011. *Bully.* Weinstein Company.

Holben, D. M., and Zirkel, P. A. 2014. School bullying litigation: An empirical analysis of the case law. *Akron Law Review* 47: 299–328.

Holt, Raczynskib, Frey, Hymel and Limber 2013 *Journal of School Violence* 12, 238–252

Horrevorts, E. M., Monshouwer, K., Wigman, J. T., Vollebergh, W. A. 2014. The relation between bullying and subclinical psychotic experiences and the influence of the bully climate of school classes. *European Child & Adolescent Psychiatry* 23 (9): 765–772. doi: 10.1007/s00787-014-0524-0.

Hong, J. S., Espelage, D. L., Grogan-Kaylor, A., and Allen-Meares, P. 2012. Identifying potential mediators and moderators of the association between child maltreatment and bullying perpetration and victimization in school. *Educational Psychology Review* 24 (2): 167–186.

Honig v. Doe (1988) 484 U.S. 305

Houghton, S. J., Nathan, E., & Taylor, M. 2012. To bully or not to bully, that is not the question: Western Australian early adolescents' in search of a reputation. *Journal of Adolescent Research* 27: 498–522.

Idsoe, T., Dyregrov, A., and Idsoe, E. C. 2012. Bullying and PTSD symptoms. 2012 *Journal of Abnormal Child Psychology* 40: 901–911.

Individuals with Disabilities Education Act, 20 U.S.C. 1400 et seq (2004).

Irby, D. J. 2013. Net-Deepening of school discipline. *The Urban Review* 197–219.

Ismail, W., Jaafar, N., Sidi, H., Midin, M., Shah, S. 2014. Why do young adolescents bully? Experience in Malaysian schools. *Comprehensive Psychiatry* 55: S114–S120.

Jacobson, R. B. 2010. On bullshit and bullying: taking seriously those we educate. *Journal of Moral Education* 39: 437–448.

Jane, Shin Park. 2014. Unfair fight. *Teen Vogue.*

Jansen, P., Verlinden, M., Dommisse-van Berkel, A., Mieloo, C., Raat., H, and Hofman, 2014. Teacher and peer reports of overweight and bullying among young primary school children. *Pediatrics.* 134: 473–480. doi: 10.1542/peds.2013-3274.

Juvonen, J., Graham, S., and Schuster, M. A. 2003. Bullying among young adolescents: The strong, the weak, and the troubled. *Pediatrics* 112: 1231–1237. doi: 10.1542/peds.112.6.1231

Kaukiainen, A., Salmivally, C., Lagerspetz, K., Tamminen, M., Vauras, M., and Maki, H. (2002). Learning difficulties, social intelligence, and self-concept: Connections to bully-victim problems. *Scandinavian Journal of Psychology* 43: 269–278.

Kim, Y. S., Leventhal, B. L., Koh, Y. J., Hubbard, A., and Boyce, W. T. 2006. School Bullying and Youth Violence: Causes or Consequences of Psychopathologic Behavior? *Arch Gen Psychiatry* 63: 1035–1041.

Klin, A., Volkmar, F., and Sparrow, S. S. (Eds.). 2000. *Asperger syndrome.* New York, NY: Guilford Press.

Kloosterman, P. J., Kelley, E. A., Craig, W. M., Parker, J. D. A., and Javier, C. 2013. Types and experiences of bullying in adolescents with an autism spectrum disorder. *Research in Autism Spectrum Disorder,* 7: 824–832.

Koenig, A. L., Cicchetti, D., and Rogosch, F. A. 2000. Child compliance/noncompliance and maternal contributors to internalization in maltreating and nonmaltreating dyads. *Child Development* 71: 1018–1032.

Kowalski, R. M., Limber, S. P., and Agatston, P. W. 2008. *Cyber Bullying: Bullying in the Digital Age.* Blackwell: Oxford, UK.

Kowalski, R. M., and Witte, J. 2006. Youth Internet Survey. http://www. camss. clemson.edu/KowalskiSurvey/servelet/Page1.

Kumpulainen, K. 2008. Psychiatric conditions associated with bullying. *International Journal of Adolescent Medicine and Health* 20 (2): 121–132.

Kumpulainen, K., Rasanen, E., and Henttonen, I. 1999. Children involved in bullying: Psychological disturbance and the persistence of the involvement. *Child Abuse & Neglect* 23: 1253–1262.

Laura, C. 2014. *Being bad: My baby brother and the school-to-prison pipeline.* New York: Teachers College Press.

Lavoie, R. (2010, April 28) *Beyond Fat City.* East Meadow SEPTA/SERCL, East Meadow, New York.

Leff, S., Power, I., and Goldstein, A. 2004. Outcome measures to assess the effectiveness of bullying prevention programs in the school. In D. Espelage & S. Swearer (Eds.) *Bullying in American schools: A social-ecological perspective on prevention and intervention* (pp. 269–293). Mahwah, NJ: Erlbaum.

Lereya, S. T., Samara, M., and Wolke, D. 2013. Parenting behavior and the risk of becoming a victim and a bully/victim: A meta-analysis study. *Child Abuse and Neglect* 37: 1091–1108.

Levin, J., and Madfis, J. 2009. Mass murder school and cumulative strain: A sequential model. *The American Behavioral Scientist* 52 (9): 1227–1245. doi: 10.1177/0002764209332543.

Leymann, H. 1990. Mobbing and psychological terror at workplaces. *Violence and Victims* 5: 119–126.

Li, Q. 2007. New bottle but old wine: A research on cyberbullying in schools. *Computers and Human Behavior* 23 (4): 1777–1791. [verified 29 Sep 2007] http://www.ucalgary.ca/~qinli/publication/cyber_chb2005.pdf.

Li, Y., Putalaz, M., and Su, Y. 2011. Interparental conflict styles and parenting behaviors: Associations with overt and relational aggression among Chinese children. *Merrill–Palmer Quarterly* 57: 402–428.

Little, L. 2002. Middle-class mothers' perceptions of peer and sibling victimization among children with Asperger's syndrome and nonverbal learning disorders. *Issues in Comprehensive Pediatric Nursing* 25 (1), 43–57. doi:10.1080/014608602753504847

Lösel, F., and Beelman, A. 2003. Effects of child skills training in preventing antisocial behavior: A systematic review of randomized evaluations. *The Annals of the American Academy of Political and Social Science* 587: 84–109. http://dx.doi.org/10.1177/0002716202250793

Lovegrove, P., Bellmore, A., Greef Green, J., Jens, K., and Ostrov, J., 2013. My voice is not going to be silent. What parents can do about children's bullying. *Journal of School Violence* 12: 253–267.

Luxenberg, H., Limber, S. P., and Olweus, D. 2014. *Bullying in U. S. Schools: 2013 Status Report*. Hazeldon Foundation.

Maag, C. 2007. December 16. When the Bullies Turned faceless. *New York Times*. www.nytimes.com/learning/teachers/featured_articles/2071218tuesday.html

Maag, J. W., and Katsiyannis, A. 2006. Behavioral intervention plans: Legal and practical considerations for students with emotional and behavioral disorders. *Behavioral Disorders* 31: 348–362.

Maag, J. W., and Katsiyannis, A. 2012. Bullying and students with disabilities: Legal and practice considerations. *Behavioral Disorders* 37: 78–86.

Marcum, C. D., Higgins, G. E., Freiburger, T. L., and Ricketts, M. L. 2013. Exploration of the cyber bullying victim/offender overlap by sex. *American Journal of Criminal Justice* 39: 538–548.

Martocci, L. 2015. *Bullying: The social destruction of self*. Philadelphia: Temple University Press.

Masi, G., Muratori, P., Manfredi, A., Lenzi, F., Polidori, L., Ruglioni, L., Milone, A. 2013. Response to treatments in youth with disruptive behavior disorders. *Comprehensive Psychiatry*, 54 (7): 1009-1015. doi:http://dx.doi.org/10.1016/j.comppsych.2013.04.00

Massachusetts Anti-Bullying Law G.L. c. 71, §370

McAdams, C. R., and Lambie, G. W. 2003. A changing profile of aggression in schools: Its impact and implications for school personnel. *Preventing School Failure* 47: 122.

McAdams, C. R., and Schmidt, C. D. 2007. How to help a bully: Recommendations for counseling the proactive aggressor, *Professional School Counseling* 11: 120–129.

McDougall, P., and Vailliancourt, T. 2015. Long-term adult outcomes of peer victimization in childhood and adolescence: Pathways to adjustment and maladjustment. *American Psychologist* 70: 300–310.

McGrath, M., and Zook, J. M. 2011. Maternal control of girls versus boys: Relations to empathy and persuasive style with peers. *Journal of Child and Family Studies.* 20: 57–65.

Melander, L. A., Hartshorn, K., and Whitbeck, L. 2013. Correlates of bullying behaviors among a sample of North American Indigenous adolescents. *Journal of Adolescence* 36: 675–684.

Melton, G. B., Limber, S. P., Cunningham, P., Osgood, D. W., Chambers, J., Flerx, V., Henggeler, S., and Nation, M. 1998. *Violence among rural youth. Final report to the office of juvenile justice and delinquency prevention.*

Merikangas, K. R., He, J., Burstein, M., Swendsen, J., Avenevoli, S., Case, B., Georgiades, K., Heaton, L., Swanson, S., and Olfson, M. 2011. Service utilization for lifetime mental disorders in U.S. adolescents: Results of the National Comorbidity Survey-Adolescent Supplement (NCS-A). *Journal of the American Academy of Child and Adolescent Psychiatry,* 50 (1): 32–45.

Merrell, K. W., Isava, D. M., Gueldner, B. A., and Ross, S. W. 2008. How effective are school bullying intervention programs? A meta-analysis of intervention research. *School Psychology Quarterly* 23: 26–42. doi: 10.1037/1045-3830.23.1.26.

Messias, E., Kindrick, K., and Castro, J. 2014. School bullying, cyber bullying, or both: Correlates of teen suicidality in the 2011 CDC youth risk behavior survey. *Comprehensive Psychiatry* 55: 1063–1068.

Meyer, E. J. 2008. Gendered harassment in secondary schools' Understanding teachers' (non) interventions. *Gender and Education* 20 (6): 555–572.

Meyer, E., and Stader, D. 2009. Queer youth and the culture wars: From the classroom to the courtroom in the United States, Canada and Australia. *Journal of GLBT Youth,* 6: 135–154.

Mikkelson, E. G., and Einarsen, S. 2002. Basic assumptions and symptoms of post-traumatic stress among victims of bullying at work. *European Journal of Work and Organizational Psychology* 11: 87–111.

Mishna, F. 2003. Learning disabilities and bullying: Double jeopardy. *Journal of Learning Disabilities* 36: 336–347.

Mitchell, K. J., Jones, L. M., Turner, H. A., Shattuck, A., & Wolak, J. (2015, June 1). The role of technology in peer harassment: Does it amplify harm for youth? *Psychology of Violence* 1–11. Advance online publication. http://dx.doi.org/10.1037/a0039317.

Modecki, K. L., Barber, B. L., and Vernon, L. 2013. Mapping developmental precursors of cyber-aggression: Trajectories of risk predict perpetration and victimization. *Journal of Youth and Adolescence* 42: 651–661.

Morrow, M. T., Hubbard, J. A., Barhight, L. J., and Thomson, A. K. 2014. Fifth-grade children's daily experiences of peer victimization and negative emotions: Moderating effects of sex and peer rejection. *Journal of Abnormal Child Psychology* 42: 1089–1102. doi:http://dx.doi.org/10.1007/s10802-014-9870-0.

Morrow, M., Hubbard, J., and Swift, L. 2014. Relations among multiple types of peer victimization, reactivity to peer victimization, and academic achievement in fifth-grade boys and girls. *Merrill–Palmer Quarterly* 60: 302–327.

Mustanoja, S., Anu-Helmi, L., Hakko, H., Rasanen, P., Saavala, H., and Riala, K. 2011. Is exposure to domestic violence and violent crime associated with bullying behaviour among underage adolescent psychiatric inpatients? *Child Psychiatry And Human Development* 42: 495–506.

Nabozny v. Podlesny (92F. 3d446.451) (7th cir) 1996.

Nansel, T. R., Overpeck, M. D., Pilla, R. S., Ruan, W. J., Simmons-Morton, B., and Scheidt, P. 2001. Bullying behavior among U.S. youth: Prevalence and association with psychosocial adjustment. *Journal of the American Medical Association* 285: 2094–2100.

National Child Traumatic Stress Network Schools Community, 2008, October. *Child Trauma toolkit for educators.* Los Angeles, CA.

National Institute of Mental Health (2011). www.nimh.nih.gov/health/.../treatment.

Navarro, R., Larranaga, E., and Yubero, S. 2010. Bullying-victimization problems and aggressive tendencies in Spanish secondary schools students: The role of gender stereotypical traits. *Social Psychology of Education* 14: 457–473.

Nekvasil, E. K., Cornell, D. G., Huang, F. L. 2015. Prevalence and offense characteristics of multiple casualty homicides: Are schools at higher risk than other locations? *Psychology of Violence*, http://dx.doi.org/10.1037/a0038967.

Nelson, J. R., Stage, S., Duppong-Hurley, K., Synhorst L., and Epstein, M. H. 2007. Risk factors predictive of the problem behavior of children at risk for emotional and behavioral disorders. *Exceptional Children* 73: 367–377.

Nelson, D. A., Yang, C., Coyne, S. M., Olsen, J. A., and Hart, C. H. 2013. Parental psychological control dimensions: Connections with Russian preschoolers' physical and relational aggression. *Journal of Applied Developmental Psychology* 34: 1–8.

Newman-Carlson, D., and Horne, A. M. 2004. Bully busters: A psychoeducational intervention for reducing bullying behavior in middle school students. *Journal of Counseling and Development* 82: 259–267.

New York State Education Department (DASA). Retrieved http:// www.p12.nysed. gov/irs/School_Safety_Summary_form_Part2.pdf.

New York State Education Department Sec 801 SS10–18.

New York State Education Department Chapter 102 Laws of 2012.

New York State Workplace Violence Prevention Act. 2006. http://www.labor.state. ny.us/workerprotection/safetyhealth.

Nicoll, W. G. 2014. Developing transformative schools: A resilience-focused paradigm for education. *International Journal of Emotional Education* 6: 47–65.

O'Connor, J. A., Graber, K. C. 2014. Sixth-grade physical education: An acculturation of bullying and fear. *Research Quarterly for Exercise and Sport* 85: 398–408.

Office for Civil Rights, U.S. Department of Education. 2010. "Dear Colleague" letter. Washington, DC: Author. Retrieved from http://www2.ed.gov/about/offices/list/ ocr/letters/colleague-2-1-1-.html

Office of Juvenile Justice Department. Bullying. Development Services Group, Inc. http://www.ojjdp.gov/mpg/litreviews/Bullying.pdf

Office of Special Education and Research, Department of Education (2013, August 30) Letter to Colleagues. http:// www2.ed.gov/policy/speced/guid/idea/ memosdcltrs/bullyingdcl-8–20–13.pdf or 61 IDELR 263 (OSERS 2013).

Offrey, L., and Rinaldi, C. 2014. Parent–child communication and adolescents' problem-solving strategies in hypothetical bullying situations. *International Journal of Adolescence and Youth.* DOI: 10.1080/02673843.2014.884006

Olweus, D. 2013. School bullying: Development and some important challenges. *Annual Review of Clinical Psychology* 9: 751–780.

Olweus, D. 1999. *In the nature of school bullying: A cross-national perspective.* In Smith, P. K., Morita Y., Junger-Tas, J, Olweus D, Catalano R, and Slee P (Eds.). Routledge: London and New York.

Olweus, D. 1998. *Aggression in the schools: Bullies and whipping boys.* Hemisphere Publishing Co.: Washington DC.

Olweus, D. 1997. Bully/victim problems in school: Fact and intervention. *European Journal of Violence Prevention* 12 (4): 495-510.

Olweus, D. 1994. Bullying at school: Basic facts and effect of a school based intervention program. *Journal of Child Psychology and Psychiatry* 35: 1171–1190.

Olweus, D. 1993. *Bullying at school: What we know and what we can do.* Oxford: Blackwell.

Olweus, D. 1993. *Victimization by peers: Antecedents and long-term outcomes.* In K. H. Rubin & J. H. B. Asendort (Eds.) Hillsdale, NJ: Erlbaum.

Olweus, D. 1991. Bully/Victim Problems Among Schoolchildren: Basic Facts and Effects of a School Based Intervention Program. In D. J. Pepler & K. H. Rubin (Eds.), *The development and treatment of childhood aggression.* Hillsdale, NJ: Erlbaum.

Oyewusi, L. M., and Orolade, K. S. 2014. Cyber bullying: A disruptive behaviour in modern day secondary school classrooms. *Journal of Educational and Social Research* 4: 421–427.

Papp, L. M. 2004. Pathways among marital distress, parental symptomatology, and child adjustment. *Journal of Marriage and Family* 66: 110–128.

Pardini, D., Stepp, S., Hipwell, A., Stouthamer-Loeber, M., and Loeber, R. 2012. The clinical utility of the proposed DSM-5 callous-unemotional subtype of conduct disorder in young girls. *Journal of the American Academy of Child and Adolescent Psychiatry* 51 (1): 62.

Patchin, J. W., and Hinduja, S. 2014. *Words wound.* Minneapolis, MN. Free Spirit Publishing.

Paul, S., Smith., P. K., and Blumberg, H. H. 2012. Comparing student perceptions of Coping strategies and school interventions in managing bullying and cyber bullying incidents. *Pastoral Care in Education* 30: 127–146.

Payne, E., and Smith, M. 2012. Rethinking Safe Schools Approaches for LGBTQ Students: Changing the Questions We Ask. *Multicultural Perspectives* 14: 187–193.

Pellegrini, A. D., and Bartini, M. 2000. An empirical comparison of methods of sampling aggression and victimization in school setting. *Journal of Educational Psychology*, 92: 360–366.

Pepler, D. J., and Craig, W. M. 2000. *Making a difference in bullying*. LaMarsh Research Centre for Violence and Conflict Resolution. Research Report 60. Toronto, Ontario: York University.

Pepler, D., Jiang, D., Craig, W., and Connolly, J. 2008. Developmental trajectories of bullying and associated factors. *Child Development* 79: 325.

Perlus, J. G., Brooks-Russell, A., Wang, J., and Iannotti, R. J. 2014. Trends in bullying, physical fighting, and weapon carrying among 6th through 10 grade students from 1998 to 2010: Findings from a national study. *American Journal of Public Health* 104 (6): 1100–1106.

Perren, S., and Alsaher, F. D. 2006. Social behavior and peer relationships of victims, bully-victims, and bullies in kindergarten. *Journal of Child Psychiatry and Psychiatry*, 47: 45–57.

Perren, S., Gutzwiller-Helfenfinger, E., Matti, T., and Hymel, S. 2011. Moral reasoning and emotional attributions of adolescent bullies, victims, and bully-victims. *British Journal of Developmental Psychology* 30: 511–530.

Perry, D. G., Kusel, S. J., and Perry, L. C. 1988. Victims of peer aggression. *Developmental Psychology* 24: 807–814.

Perry, D., Williard, J., and Perry, L. 1990. Peers' perceptions of the consequences that victimized children provide aggressors, *Child Development* 61: 1289–1309.

Pillemer, K., Chen, E. K., Van Haitsma, K. S., Teresi, J., Ramirez, M., Silver, S., and Lachs, M. S. 2012. Resident-to-Resident Aggression in Nursing Homes: Results from a Qualitative Event Reconstruction Study. *The Gerontologist* 52 (1), 24–33. doi:10.1093/geront/gnr107.

Pinkelman, S. E., McIntosh, K. Rasplica, C. K., Berg, T., and Strickland-Cohen, M. 2015. Perceived enablers and barriers related to sustainability of school-wide positive behavioral interventions and supports. *Behavioral Disorders* 40 (3): 171–183. http://0-search.proquest.com.library.dowling.edu/docview/1693347913?accountid=10549.

Popp, A., Peguero A. A., Day, K. R., and Kahle, L. L. 2014. Gender, bullying victimization, and education. *Violence and Victims* 29: 843–856.

Poteat, V. P., Mereish, E. H., DiGiovanni, C. D., and Koenig, B. W. 2011. The effects of general and homophobic victimization on adolescents' psychosocial and educational concerns: The importance of intersecting identities and parent support. *Journal of Counseling Psychology*, 58: 597–609. doi:10.1037/a0025095.

Pousels, J. L., and Cillessen, A. H. N. 2013. Correlates and outcomes associated with aggression and victimization among elementary-school children in a low-income urban context. *Journal of Youth and Adolescence* 42: 190–205.

Poyhonen, V., Juvonen, J., and Salmivalli, C. 2010. What does it take for the victim of bullying? The interplay between personal and social factors. *Merrill-Palmer Quarterly* 56:143–163.

Preston, J. June 22, 2012. *New York Times*. For bullied bus monitor, a windfall to ease the pain. http://www.nytimes.com/2012/06/23/nyregion/for-bullied-bus-monitor-funds- raised-to-take-hurt-away.html?_r=0

Pritchard, E. D. 2013. For colored kids who committed suicide, our outrage isn't enough: Queer youth of color, bullying, and the discursive limits of identity and safety. *Harvard Educational Review* 83: 320–345, 401–402.

Quammen, D. August, 2014. Gombe family album. *National Geographic* 226 (2): 52–65.

Rahey, L., and Craig, W. M. 2002. Evaluation of an ecological program to reduce bullying in schools. *Canadian Journal of Counseling* 36: 281–297.

Raven, S., and Jurkiewicz, M. A. 2014. Preservice secondary Science teachers' experience and ideas about bullying in science classrooms. *Science Educator* 23: 65–72.

Reid, J., Patterson, G., and Snyder, J. 2002. *Antisocial behavior in children and adolescents: A developmental analysis and model of intervention.* Washington, DC: American Psychological Association.

Reijntjes, A., Vermande, M., Olthof, T., Goossens, F. A., van de Schoot, R., Aleva, L., and van der Meulen, M. 2013. Costs and benefits of bullying in the context of the peer group: A three wave longitudinal analysis. *Journal of Abnormal Child Psychology* 41: 1217–1229.

Rigby, K. 2012. Bullying is schools: Addressing desires, not only behaviours. *Education Psychological Review*, 24, 339–348.

Rigby, K. 1994. Psychosocial functioning in families of Australian adolescent schoolchildren involved in bully/victim problems. *Journal of Family Therapy*, 16: 173–187.

Rigby, K. 1993. School children's perceptions of their families and parents as a function of peer relations. *The Journal of Genetic Psychology*, 154: 501–513.

Rigby, K., and Slee, P. T. 1991. Bullying among Australian school children: Reported behavior and attitudes to victims. *Journal of Social Psychology* 13: 615–627.

Robers, S., Kemp, J., Rathbun, A., and Morgan, R. E. 2014. *Indicators of School Crime and Safety: 2013* (NCES 2014–042/NCJ 243299). National Center for Education Statistics, U.S. Department of Education, and Bureau of Justice Statistics, Office of Justice Programs, U.S. Department of Justice. Washington, DC. Retrieved from http:nces.ed/gov/pubs2014/2014042.pdf

Rodkin, P. C., Espelage, D. L., and Hanish, L. D. 2015. A relational framework for understanding bullying: Developmental antecedents and outcomes. *American Psychologist* 70: 311–321.

Rodkin, P. C. 2012. Bullying and children's peer relationships. *Education Matters*, 8, 2.

Rose, C. A., Espelage, D. L., Aragon, S. R., and Elliott, J. 2011. Bullying and victimization among students in special education and general education curricula. *Exceptionality Education International*, 21: 2–14.

Rose, C. A., Monda-Amaya, L. E., and Espelage, D. L. 2011. Bullying perpetration and victimization in special education: A review of the literature. *Remedial and Special Education*, 32: 114–130.

Rubin, M. 2002. Youth bullying: An overview. *Educational Forum on Adolescent Health*.

Ryan, W., and Smith, D. J. 2009. Anti-bullying programs in schools: How effective are evaluation practices? *Prevention Science* 10: 248–266.

Salmivalli, C., Kaukianinen, A., Kaistaniemi, L., and Lagerspetz, K. 1999. Self-evaluated self-esteem, peer-evaluated self-esteem, and defensive egotism as predictors of adolescents' participation in bullying situations. *Personality and Social Psychology Bulletin* 25: 1268–1278. doi: 10.1177/0146167299258008.

Salmivalli, C., Lagerspetz, K., Bjorkqvist, K., Osterman, K., and Kaukiainen, A. 1996. Bullying as a group process: Participant roles and their relations to social status within the group. *Aggressive Behavior* 22: 1–5.

Salmon, G., James, A., and Smith, D. M. 1998. Bullying in schools: Self reported anxiety, depression, and self esteem in secondary school children. *British Medical Journal* 317: 924–925.

Salwina, W., Ismail, W., Uzyanei, N., Jaafar, N., Sidi, H., Midin, M., and Shah, S.A. 2014. Why do young adolescents bully? Experience in Malaysian schools. *Comprehensive Psychiatry* 55: S114–S120.

Scott, S., Sylva, K., Doolan, M., Price, J., Jacobs, B., Crook, C., and Landau, S. 2010. Randomized controlled trial of parent groups for child antisocial behavior targeting multiple risk factors: The spokes project. *Child Psychology and Psychiatry* 51: 48–57. doi: 10.1111/j.1469-7610.2009.02127.

Shahani, A. 2015, July 13. National Public Radio. On College campuses, suicide intervention via anonymous app. www.npr.org/sections/alltechconsidered/2015/07/13/422620195/.

Shearer, L. 2015. State program segregates behavior-disabled students. Online Anthens.

Shetgiri, R., Lin, H., and Flores, G. 2013. Trends in risk and protective factors for child bullying perpetration in the United States. *Child Psychiatry and Human Development* 44 (1): 89–104. doi:http://dx.doi.org/10.1007/s10578-012-0312-3.

Shetgiri, R., Lin, H., and Flores, G. 2012. Identifying children at risk for being bullies in the United States. *Academic Pediatrics* 12: 509–522.

Shireen, F., Janapana, H., Rehmatullah, S. Temuri, H., and Azim, F. 2014. Trauma experience of youngsters and teens: A key issue in suicidal behavior among victims of bullying? *Pak J Med Sci* 30 (1): 206–210.

Shields, A., and Cicchetti, D. 2001. Parental maltreatment and emotional dysregulation as risk factors for bullying and victimization in middle childhood. *Journal of Clinical Child Psychology* 30: 349–363.

Shtayermman, O. 2007. Peer victimization in adolescents and young adults diagnosed with Asperger's Syndrome: a link to depressive symptomatology, anxiety symptomatology and suicidal ideation. *Issues in Comprehensive Pediatric Nursing* 30: 87–107.

Siegel, R. (July 13, 2015). An app to stop cyberbullying. National Public Radio: All Things Considered. www.npr.org/20150/07/13/422672888/an-app-to-stop-cyberbullying

Sijtsema, J. J., Veenstra, R., Lindenberg, S., and Salmivalli, C. 2009. Empirical test of bullies' status goals: assessing direct goals, aggression, and prestige. *Aggressive Behavior* 35: 57–67.

Sinyor, M., Schaffer, A., and Amy H Cheung, A. 2014. An observational study of bullying as a contributing factor in youth suicide in Toronto. *Canadian Journal of Psychiatry* 59 (12): 632–638.

Skiba, R. J., and Peterson, R. L. 2000. School discipline at a crossroads: From zero tolerance to early response. *Exceptional Children* 66: 335.

Smith, P. 2000. Bullying and harassment in schools and the rights of children. *Children and Society* 14: 294–303.

Smith, P. K., Kupferberg, A., Mora-Merchan, J. A., Samara, M., Bosley, S., and Osborn, R. 2012. A content analysis of school anti-bullying policies: A follow-up after six years. *Educational Psychology in Practice* 28: 47–70.

Smith, J. D., Schneider, B. H., Smith, P. K., and Ananiadou, K. 2004. The effectiveness of whole-school anti-bullying programs: A synthesis of evaluation research. *School Psychology Review* 33: 547–560.

Smith, P. K., and Sharp, S. 1994. *Bullying at school.* London: Routledge.

Solomon, A. 2014 March 17. The father of the Sandy Hook Killer searches for answers. The reckoning. *The New Yorker: Annals of Psychology.*http://www. newyorker.com/reporting/2014/03/17/140317fa_fact_solomon?intable=true&curr entPage=all

Son, E., Peterson, N., Pottick, K. J. Zippay, A., Parish, S. L., and Lohrmann, S. 2014. Peer victimization among young children with disabilities: Early risk and protective factors. *Exceptional Children* 80: 368–384.

Sourander, A., Jensen, P., Rönning, J. A., Niemelä, S., Helenius, H., Sillanmäki, L., and Almqvist, F. 2007. What is the early adulthood outcome of boys who bully or are bullied in childhood? The Finnish "From a Boy to a Man" study. *Pediatrics*, 120: 397–404.

Srabstein, J. C., and Leventhal, B. L. 2010. Prevention of bullying-related morbidity and mortality: A call for public health policies. *Bulletin of the World Health Organization* 88: 403–403. Doi: 10.2471/BLT.10.077123

State of Connecticut Department of Criminal Justice. November 25, 2013. A Report by Stephen J. Sedensky III, the State's Attorney, from the Office of the State's Attorney Judicial District of Danbury.

State of Massachusetts. 38, Section 72. July 1, 2013

Stellwagen, K., and Kerig, P. 2012. Ringleader bullying: Association with psychopathic narcissism and theory of mind among child psychiatric inpatients. *Child Psychiatry & Human Development* 44 (5): 612–620. doi 10.1007/s10578-012-0355-5.

Sterzing, P. R., Shattuck, P. T., Narendorf, S.C., Wagner, M., and Cooper, B. P. 2012. Prevalence and correlates of Bullying involvement among adolescents with an Autism Spectrum disorder. *Ach Pediatric Adolesc Med* 66 (11): 1058–1064. doi: 10.1001/archpediatrics.2012.790

Stavrinides, P., Nikiforou, M., and Georgiou, S. 2014. Do mothers know? Longitudinal associations between parental knowledge, bullying, and victimization. *Journal of Social and Personal Relationships.* published online 6 March 2014 DOI: 10.1177/0265407514525889

Student Non-Discrimination Act of 2011: H.R. 998 (112th)

Sugai, G., and Horner, R. R. 2006. A promising approach for expanding and sustaining school-wide positive behavior support. *School Psychology Review* 35: 245–259.

Suler, J. 2004. The online disinhibition effect. *CyberPsychology & Behavior* 7: 321–326.

Sutton, J., Smith, P., and Swettenham, J. 1999. Social cognition and bullying: Social inadequacy or skilled manipulation? *British Journal of Developmental Psychology* 17: 435–450.

Swearer, S., and Espelage, D. L. 2004. Introduction: A social-ecological framework of bullying among youth. *Bullying in American schools: A social-ecological perspective on prevention and intervention*, In Espelage, D. L., and Swearer, S. M. (Eds.). 2004. Lawrence Erlbaum Associates: New Jersey.

Swearer, S. M., Espelage, D. L., Vaillancourt, T., and Hymel, S. 2010. What can be done about school bullying? Linking research to educational practice. *Educational Researcher* 39 (1): 38–47.

Swearer, S., and Hymel, S. 2015. Understanding the psychology of bullying. *American Psychologist* 344–353.

Swearer, S. M., Wang, C., Collins, Strawhun, J., and Fluke, S. 2014. Bullying: A school mental health perspective. In M. D. Weiss, Lever, Bradshaw and El? (Eds.). Handbook of School Mental Health: Advancing Practice and Research 2nd ed. Springer Science+Business Media: New York., pp. 341–354.

Talbot, M. 2002 February 24. Girls just want to be mean. *New York Times Magazine,* 24–65.

Takizawa, R., Danese, A., Maughan, B., and Arseneault, L. 2015. Bullying victimization in childhood predicts inflammation and obesity at mid-life: a five-decade birth cohort study. *Psychological Medicine* 1–11. doi:10.1017/S0033291715000653.

Tinker v. DesMoines Independent Community School District1969 393 U.S. 503.

Title II of the American with Disabilities Act of 1990 (Title II), 42 U.S.C. 12131.

Title IX of the Education Amendments of 1972 (Title IX), 20 U.S.C. 1681.

Title VI of the Civil Rights Act of 1964 (Pub. L 88–352, 78 Stat. 241).

Tippett, N., Wolke, D., and Platt, L. 2013. Ethnicity and bullying involvement in a national UK youth sample. *Journal of Adolescence* 36: 639–649.

Tippett, N., and Wolke, D. 2014. Socioeconomic status and bullying: A meta-analysis. *American Journal of Public Health* 104: e48–e59. doi:10.2105/AJPH.2014.301960

Towl, P. 2014. Would the real bully please stand up. *New Zealand Journal of Educational Studies* 49: 59–71.

Ttofi, M. M., and Farrington, D. P., 2011. Effectiveness of school based programs to reduce bullying: A system and meta-analytic review. *Journal of Experimental Criminology* 7: 27–56.

Ttofi, M. M., Farrington, D. P., and Lösel, F. 2014. Interrupting the continuity from school bullying to later internalizing and externalizing problems: Findings from cross-national comparative Studies, *Journal of School Violence* 13: 1–4. doi: 10.1080/15388220.2013.857346

Tudkuea, T., and Laeheem, K. 2014. Development of indicators of cyber bullying among youths in Songkhla province. *Asian Social Science* 10: 74–80.

Tulley, D. January–February 2009. Response to intervention: 21 Questions and answers just what is RTI, 2011 Lucky 21). 50 (4).

Turner, H. A., Finkelhor, D., Hamby, S. L., Anne Shattuck, A., and Ormrod R. K. 2011. Specifying type and location of peer victimization in a national sample of children.

Undheim, A. M. 2013. Involvement in bullying as predictor of suicidal ideation among 12- to 15-year-old Norwegian adolescents. *European Child & Adolescent Psychiatry* 22: 357–365. doi 10.1007/s00787-012-0373-7

Undheim, A. M., and Sund, A. M. 2010. Prevalence of bullying and aggressive behavior and their relationship to mental health problems among 12- to 15-year-old Norwegian adolescents. *European Children Psychiatry,* 19: 803–811.

20 U.S.C. § 1400 The Individuals with Disabilities Education Act.

29 U.S. C. § 794 Section 504 of the Rehabilitation Act.

20 U.S.C. § 1232 The Family Educational and Privacy Rights Act.

United States Commission on Civil Rights. *Peer-to-peer violence + Bullying: Examining the federal responses.* Sept. 2011. Washington DC. www.usccr.gov.

United States Department of Education. 2013. Letter to Colleagues. http:// www2. ed.gov/policy/speced/guid/idea/memosdcltrs/ bullyingdcl-8–20–13.pdf or 61IDELR 263 (OSERS 2013).

University of the State of New York. The State Education Department (2010). Albany, New York: Office for Civil Rights, "Dear Colleague" letter. Washington, DC.

Vaillancourt, T., Hymel, S., and McDougall, P. 2003. Bullying is power: Implications for school-based intervention strategies. *Journal of Applied School Psychology* 19: 157–176.

Vaillancourt, T., Trinh, V., McDougall, P., Duku, E., Cunningham, L., Cunningham, C., Short, K. 2010. Optimizing population screening of bullying in school-aged Children. *Journal of School Violence* 9: 233–250.

Vaughn, M. G., DeLisi, M., Gunter, T., Fu, Q., Beaver, K. M., Perron, B. E., and Howard, M. O. 2011. The severe 5%: A latent class analysis of the externalizing behavior spectrum in the United States. *Journal of Criminal Justice* 39: 75–80.

Vaughn, M. G., Fu, Q., Bender, K., DeLisi, M., Beaver, K. M., Perron, B. E., and Howard, M. O. 2010. Psychiatric correlates of bullying in the United States: Findings from a national sample. *Psychiatr Q* 81: 183–195.

Velki, T. 2012. A comparison of individual characteristics and the multiple contexts for children with different bullying status: An ecological perspective. *International Journal of Arts & Sciences* 5: 89–112.

Veenstra, R. Lindenberg, S., Zijlstra, B. J. H., De Winter, A. F., Verhulst, F. C., and Ormel, J. 2007. The Dyadic Nature of Bullying and Victimization: Testing a Dual-Perspective Theory. *Child Development* 78: 1843–1854.

Viding, E., Simmonds, E., Petrides, K.V., and Frederickson, N. 2009. The contribution of callous-unemotional traits and conduct problems to bullying in early adolescence. *Journal of Child Psychology and Psychiatry* 50: 471–481.

Vlachou, M., Andreou, E., Botsoglou, K., Didaskalou, E. 2001. Bully/victim problems among preschool children: A review of current research evidence. *Educational Psychology Review* 23 (3): 329–358.

Vossekuil, B., Fein, R. A., Reddy, M., Borum, R., and Modzeleski,W. 2002. *The final report and findings of the safe school initiative: Implications for the prevention of school attacks in the United States.* Washington DC: U.S. Secret Service and U.S. Department of Education.

Vreeman, R. C., and Carroll, A. E. 2007. A systematic review of school-based interventions to prevent bullying. *Archives of Pediatric and Adolescent Medicine* 161: 78–88.

Wagner, M., Kutash, K., Duchnowski, A. J., and Epstein, M. H. 2005. The Special Education Elementary Longitudinal Study and the National Longitudinal Transition Study: Study designs and implications for children with emotional disturbance. *Journal of Emotional and Behavioral Disorder* 13: 25–41. doi: 10:1177/10634266050130010301

Walker, H., and Severson, H. 1990. Systematic screening for behavior disorders (SSBD). Longmont, CO: Sopris West.

Wang, J., Iannotti, R. J., and Nansel, T. R. 2009. School bullying among adolescents in the United States: Physical, verbal, relational, and cyber. *Journal of Adolescent Health* 45: 368–375.

Waasdorp, T. E., Bradshaw, C. P. 2015. The overlap between cyberbullying and traditional bullying. *Journal of Adolescent Health* 56 (5): 483–488.

Weatherly, J. J. 2012. *Lucky 21*, 50–52, Council of Administrators of Special Education: Warner Robins, GA.

Webster-Stratton, C. 1996. Early-onset conduct problems: Does gender make a difference? *Journal of Consulting and Clinical Psychology*, 64: 540–551.

Wei, H., and Lee, W. 2014. Individual and social network predictors of physical bullying: A Longitudinal study of Taiwanese early adolescents. *Violence and Victims* 29: 701–16.

Welton, E., Vakil, S., and Ford, B. 2014. Beyond bullying: Consideration of additional research for the assessment and prevention of potential rampage school violence in the United States. *Education Research International.*

White, S. F., Frick, P. J., Lawing, K., and Bauer, D. 2013. Callous-Unemotional traits and response to functional family therapy in adolescent offenders. *Behavioral Sciences and the Law* 31: 271–285.

White House Conference on Bullying Prevention. March 10, 2011. The White House.

Whitney, I., and Smith, P.K. 1993. A survey of the nature and extent of bullying in junior/middle and secondary schools. *Educational Research* 35: 3–25.

Wiley, L. H. 1999. Pretending to be Normal: Living with Asperger Syndrome. Jessica Kingsley Publishers: London.

Willard, N. 2005. Educator's Guide to Cyberbullying Addressing the Harm Caused by Online Social Cruelty. Center for Safe and Responsible Internet Use. http://www.embracecivility.org.

Wolfson, A. 2015. March 23 Are schools liable in suicides? Ky high court hears case. USA Today.

Wolke, D., Copeland, W. E., Angold, A., and Jane Costello, E. J. 2013. Impact of bullying in childhood on adult health, wealth, crime, and social outcomes, *Psychological Science.* doi: 10.1177/0956797613481608

Wolke, D., Lereya, S. T., Fisher, H. L., Lewis, G., and Zammit, S. 2014. Bullying in elementary school and psychotic experiences at 18 years: A longitudinal, population-based cohort study. *Psychological Medicine* 44: 2199–211.

Worley, S. 2015. After trauma, helping children and adolescents heal. *Penn Medicine* 8–15.

Yang, S. Stewart, R., Kim, J., Kim, S., Shin, I. et al. 2013. Differences in predictors of traditional and cyber-bullying: A 2-year longitudinal study in Korean school children. *European Child and Adolescent Psychiatry* 22 (5): 309–18.

Yen, C., Yang, P., Wang, P., Lin, H., Liu, T., Wu, Y., and Tang, T. 2014. Association between school bullying levels /types and mental health problems among Taiwanese adolescents, *Comprehensive Psychiatry* 55: 405–413.

Yoshikawa, H., Weiland, C., Brooks-Gunn, J., Burchinal, M., Espinosa, L., Gormley, W., and Zaslow, M. J. 2013. Investing in our future: The evidence base for preschool education. *Policy brief, Society for Research in Child Development and the Foundation for Child Development.* Retrieved from the Foundation for Child Development website: fcd-us.org/sites/default/files/Evidence Base on Preschool Education FINAL.pdf.

Zablotsky, B., Bradshaw, C. P., Anderson, C., and Law, P. 2013. The association between bullying and the psychological functioning of children with autism spectrum disorders. *Journal of Developmental and Behavioral Pediatrics* 34: 1–8.

Zwierzynska, K., Wolke, D., and Lereya, T. S., 2013. Peer victimization in childhood and internalizing problems in adolescence: A prospective longitudinal study. *Journal of Abnormal child Psychology* 41: 309–323.

Index

About the Author

Susan Carter developed an interest in school bullying through experience as a teacher and school district administrator in the states of Massachusetts, Connecticut, and New York. She is an Associate Professor of Special Education and Department Chairperson at Dowling College, Oakdale, Long Island, New York, and an approved New York State Dignity for All Students (DASA) provider teaching anti-bullying and harassment workshops. She has published in *Issues in Comprehensive Pediatric Nursing, Excelsior, Leadership in Teaching and Learning, and the Journal of Special Education Leadership*, serves as a journal reviewer for *Pediatrics, Journal of Autism and Developmental Disorders, Teaching Exceptional Children*, and has presented at conferences across the country.

Dr. Carter received an Ed. D. and M. Ed. in Administration and Supervision of Special Education from Teachers College, Columbia University, Diploma in Professional Education from the University of Connecticut, and Bachelors and Masters Degrees from Springfield College, Massachusetts. Her work *Comparison of Children and Adolescents with Asperger Syndrome to Their Peers with Learning Disabilities in Adaptive Functioning, Academic Achievement, and Victimization* was published in *Dissertation Abstracts International*, 66 (01) UMI. No. 3160618 (2005) and explored the problem of victimization in students with Asperger syndrome. She is a member of the Council of Administrators of Special Education (CASE), Council for Exceptional Children (CEC), Long Island Association of Special Education Administrators (LIASEA), and Kappa Delta Pi International Honor Society.

Lightning Source UK Ltd.
Milton Keynes UK
UKOW01n0802030816

279849UK00009B/160/P